Hymns to the Gods

Also from Westphalia Press
westphaliapress.org

Hymns to the Gods

and Other Poems

by Gen. Albert Pike

WESTPHALIA PRESS
An imprint of Policy Studies Organization

Hymns to the Gods and Other Poems
All Rights Reserved © 2014 by Policy Studies Organization

Westphalia Press
An imprint of Policy Studies Organization
1527 New Hampshire Ave., NW
Washington, D.C. 20036
info@ipsonet.org

ISBN-13: 978-1633910423
ISBN-10: 1633910423

Cover design by Taillefer Long at Illuminated Stories:
www.illuminatedstories.com

Daniel Gutierrez-Sandoval, Executive Director
PSO and Westphalia Press

Devin Proctor, Director of Media and Publications
PSO and Westphalia Press

Updated material and comments on this edition
can be found at the Westphalia Press website:
www.westphaliapress.org

HYMNS TO THE GODS
AND OTHER POEMS

by

GEN. ALBERT PIKE

EDITED BY MRS. LILIAN PIKE ROOME
Daughter of the Author

ILLUSTRATED

LITTLE ROCK, ARKANSAS
FRED W. ALLSOPP
1916

HERA

CONTENTS

HYMNS TO THE GODS AND OTHER POEMS

HYMNS TO THE GODS.

No. 1.

TO HÉRA.

I.

Mother of Gods! devoutly we incline
Our willing knees before thy holy shrine,
Where Imbrasus runs seaward, strong and swift,
Through the green plains of Samos. Lo! we lift
Gladly to thee our many-voiced strain,
Sung never to thy Majesty in vain.
The day wears on; the expanding sun stoops low;
While, in the east, thy Messenger's bent bow
Gladdens the eyes of eager worshippers.
A soft, sweet wind thy garlands lightly stirs,
Where thy loved flowers, dear Queen of Heaven, Divine!
White lilies with the dittany entwine,
And the gay poppy. Wilt thou deign to hear
Our solemn chant—loud, earnest, and sincere—
And grant our prayer? Come from Olympus down,
In regal glory, with thy starry crown,
And sceptre flashing with great gems, whereon
Thy cuckoo broods! Let not the reluctant sun
Dip in the sea, before our glad eyes greet
The distant glitter of thy snowy feet,

   Sandaled with ivory,

That shame the fairest of our green isle's daughters,
  And flash upon the undulating sea,
Like rays of star-light on a blue meer's slumbering waters!

II.

Power, Empire, Virtue,—these are thy gift;
Inspired by thee, low men their eyes uplift,
As hawks to the sun, and aim at high estate,
And reach it; while the mighty and the great,
Toppling like towers, fall headlong. By thee urged,
Men in the sloughs of wretchedness immerged
Arm them anew with courage resolute,
Bear pain and evil with endurance mute,
And grow divine in virtuous fortitude.
Woman, by thee with constancy endued,
In ill report and evil fortune clings
More closely to her husband's side, and brings
Her lovely patience ever to his aid
In the world's fierce trials. Power and Empire fade
And are dissolved like a thin April cloud;
But Virtue is immortal. Men have bowed
A thousand years before thy lofty shrines,
Clamoring for Power; but rarely one inclines,
In prayer for Virtue, Truth and Constancy,
Before thine altars the obsequious knee.
  We, prostrate at thy feet,
Of these—the only true and priceless treasure—
  Do humbly and beseechingly entreat
Thy Majesty benign to grant us ample measure.

"Power, Empire, Virtue,—these are thy gifts;
Inspired by thee, low men their eyes uplift."

III.

Where tarriest thou, Cithæronæa, now?—
Perhaps, upon some mountain's regal brow—
Cyllene or Oromedon—reclined,
No cares of state disturbing thy great mind,
Thou gazest on our lovely Grecian isles,
Along whose shores the tranquil ocean smiles
Serene as thou: around thee hoary firs
Swing their tall heads, and many an old beech stirs.
And, dreaming, murmurs, and the grave oaks spread
Their leafy limbs; and, watching overhead,
Thy kingly hawk, scarce móving his wide wings,
Rocked by the mountain-breezes, idly swings:
Perhaps in some secluded, shady nook,
On the green margin of a happy brook,
Lulled by its music into tranquil sleep,
While thy young Nymphs demurely round thee keep
Their patient vigil.   In whatever spot
Of rarest beauty,—cave, lawn, dell, or grot,
Cool glade, deep vale, or silver-sanded shore,
Or river-bank shaded with sycamore,—
     Hearken, oh, lovely Queen!
To the loud echo of our plaintive voices:
     Approach us while the laughing Earth is green,
And the young Spring in buds and golden flowers rejoices.

7

IV.

Oh, Queen! beloved of all the laughing Hours,
Let snowy-shouldered Hebe, crowned with flowers,
Before the rising of the evening-star,
Harness the peacocks to thy jewelled car:
Leave, for a time, the mighty Thunderer's side,
And thy swift birds let dextrous Iris guide
To our fair shore. Stay not thy flashing wheels
On the dark Euxine, ploughed with many keels,
Or where the vexed Propontis hoarsely swells;
In Cos, or Naxos, or the Arcadian dells;
Come, Heaven's wonder! come to our island, first;
Where thou wast born, and by the Seasons nursed!
By those sweet hours when all thy virgin charms
Were first encircled by Jove's mighty arms,—
When thy large eyes, magnificently bright,
Looked into his with soft and loving light,
And, on his breast hiding thy blushing face,
Thou hadst no peer in loveliness and grace,—
By those sweet hours, come! while the sun yet slides
Down the sky's slant, and bless these innocent brides,
    Who watch the western sky,
Their breasts with fear and rapture palpitating:
    Come! thou, who must their virgin zones untie,
Lest they, despairing, weep, and faint with longer waiting.

1845.

TO POSEIDÓN.

I.

God of the mighty deep! wherever now
The waves beneath thy brazen axles bow;
Whether thy strong, proud steeds, wind-winged and wild,
Trample the storm-vexed waters round then piled,
Swift as the lightning flashes that reveal
The quick gyrations of each massive wheel,—
While round and under thee, with hideous roar,
The broad Atlantic, with thy scourging sore,
Thundering like antique Chaos in his spasms.
In heaving mountains and deep-yawning chasms,
Fluctuates endlessly; while through the gloom,
Their glossy sides and thick manes flecked with foam,
Career thy coursers, neighing with mad glee,
In fierce response to the tumultuous sea:—
Whether they tread the sounding sands below,
Among wrecked ships, where the green sea-plants grow,
Broad-leaved, and sighing with eternal motion
Over the pale, cold tenants of the ocean:
Oh, come! our lofty altars for thee stand,
Smoking with incense, on the level strand.

II.

Perhaps with loose rein now thy horses roam
Over the Adriatic. No salt foam
Stains their fine limbs, but softly, leisurely,
They tread with silver feet that still, calm sea,
Fanning the waters with their floating manes,
That gleam like mist in sunshine; while shrill strains
From clamorous trumpets round thy chariot ring,
And green-robed sea-gods praising thee, their king,
Chaunt loudly; while Apollo bends his gaze
Lovingly on thee, and his soft clear rays
Tame thy wild coursers' eyes. The air feels warm
On the sea's forehead, where the cold, harsh storm
So lately thundered, and the rebel winds
That Æolus in cave and den now binds,
Beat their broad wings. Perhaps long leagues below
Thou sleepest in green caves, where sea-flowers glow
Brighter than sapphires: many a monster cumbers
The sand around thee; aged Triton slumbers
Care-free and still; and glad, sweet, bright eyes peep
From many a nook, watching thy dreamless sleep.

III.

Perhaps thou art resting on some Indian isle,
Under a broad, thick tree, where, many a mile.
Stretches a sunny shore, with golden sands,
Piled in fantastic shapes by Naiads' hands;
Where the small waves come coyly, one by one,
And curl upon the beach, like molten gold,
Thick-set with jewellery rare and old,
Sea-nymphs sit near, and with small delicate shells
Make thee such melody, as in deep dells,
Of a May-night, is by the Fairies made,
When, frolicking within some sober shade,
They sound their silver flutes, soft, faint, and sweet,
In strange but exquisite tunes; and delicate feet
Dance softly on the grass-blades gemmed with dew,
That bend, not break: all wanton airs that blew
So lately through the spice-trees, hover there,
With overladen wings that loan to the air
Wealth of perfume. Oh! wilt thou not arise,
And come with them to our new sacrifice?

1829.

11

TO DĒMĒTĒR.

I.

Goddess of bounty! at whose spring-time call,
When on the dewy earth thy first tones fall,
And echo in its heart, each young green blade
Springs, wondering, into life; the dull, gray glade
Is liveried with new grass,—from each chill hole,
Where they had nestled, dumb, and dull of soul,
The glad birds come, and sing for joy to thee,
Among the thronging leaves; and fast and free
The rivers run, crushing their icy chains,
Broken by thee and by thine April rains,
Through green clad valleys: Thou who chiefly art
The Goddess of all beauty,—thou whose heart
Is ever in the sunny meads and fields,—
To whom the laughing earth looks up, and yields
Her choicest treasures: Thou, that in thy car,
Drawn by winged dragons, when the morning star
Sheds his cool light, dost touch the budding trees,
And all their blossoms woo the trembling breeze;
　　Oh! pour thy light
　　Of truth and joy upon our souls tonight,
And grant to us great plenty and sweet ease!

12

II.

Benignant Goddess of the rustling corn!
Thou to whom reapers sing, and on the lawn
Bind up gigantic sheaves of full-eared wheat;
While innocent maids, with little, dancing feet,
Bring thee gay poppies, weave for thee a crown
Of modest flowers, and gracefully bend down
To garland thy full baskets; at whose side,
Among the sheaves, young Bacchos loves to ride,
With bright, clear, sparkling eyes, and feet and mouth
All wine-stained in the glad and sunny south!
Perhaps ye ride among the leafy vines,
While round thy neck one rosy arm he twines,
And with the other hand still gathers up
And presses the plump grapes, and holds the cup
To thy loved lips, then throws aside the wine,
And crowns thee with the green leaves of the vine,
Kisses thy brow, thy mouth, thine eyes most bright
With love and joy. If those dear eyes now light
    Some favored hill
    Of vine-clad Thrace, oh! come, while all is still,
And with them bless the coming of this night!

III.

Lo! the small stars rise from the silver ocean,
And wander up the sky. A sweet emotion

Stirs the white bosoms of the thin, soft clouds;
And the light mist, that the gray hills enshrouds,
Gleams like a rain of diamonds in the air.
Lo! a soft blush of light is rising there,
Like silver shining through a tint of red;
And soon the queenly moon her love will shed
Like pearl-mist on the islands and the sea,
Which thou wilt cross to view our mystery.
Lo! we have torches here for thee, and urns,
Where incense with delicious odor burns,
On altars piled with glowing fruit, as sweet
And ripe as thy sweet lips; with yellow wheat,
Flowers gathered while the Dawn lay half-asleep.
And Indian spices: patiently we keep
Our earnest watch for thee, bending before
Thy waiting altars, till to our fair shore
    Thy chariot-wheels
    Shall roll, while Ocean to the burden reels,
And utters to the sky a stifled roar.

1830.

TO DIÓNŪSOS

Where art thou, Dionusos?   On the hills
Of some fair land afar, where sweet wine fills
The clustered grapes, dost stain thy ripe lips red
With rich old juice, that men long ages dead—
Thy votaries—pressed and hid?   Dost thou hold up
'Twixt thee and the sun thy jewel-cinctured cup,
With luminous rubies brimmed?   Or doth thy car,
Lit by the blaze of the far northern star,
Roll over Thracia's hills, while all around
Shout thy mad bacchanals, and rings the sound
Of merry revelry, and distant men
Start at thy clamor?   Or in some cool glen
Reclinest thou, under dark ivy leaves,
Idling the day off, while each mad Faun weaves
Gay garlands for thee, sipping a great bowl
Of stout, strong wine; and the dismaying roll
Of thy all-conquering wheels no more is heard,
But thy strong tigers, with no fierce dream stirred,
       Crouch at thy feet?
       Iacchos! come to meet
Thy worshippers, that here with merry word
Of olden song thy godhead long to greet.

II.

Oh, thou who lovest pleasure! at whose heart
Wine's warmth is always felt; who takest part
In all mad, wanton mirth; who in the dance
Of merry maidens joinest, where the glance
Of bright black eyes, and twinkling of white feet,
Of lovely girls delight thee, when they meet
Under the summer moon!—Giver of peace
To all careworn, sad men!—whose smiles make cease
The piercing pains of grief; for whom young maids
Weave ivy garlands, and in pleasant glades
Hang up thine image, and, with happy looks,
Go dancing round, while shepherds, with long crooks,
Join the glad company, and glide about
With merry laugh and many a hearty shout,
Staining with rich dark grapes each little cheek
That most they love; and then with sudden freak,
Seizing the willing hand, and dancing on
About the green mound:—Oh, thou merry son
    Of supreme JOVE!
    Wherever thou dost rove,
Among the thick vines, come, ere day is done,
And let us too thy sunny influence prove.

III.

Where art thou, CONQUEROR!—before whom fell
The jewelled kings of Ind, when the strong swell
Of thy great multitudes came on them, and
The mystic thursos in thy red right hand
Was shaken over them, till every soul
Grew faint, as smit with lightning; when the roll
Of thy great chariot-wheels was on the neck
Of mighty potentates; till thou didst check
Thy tigers and wild lynxes on the shore
Of the Indian sea, and still its angry roar
With sparkling and delicious Grecian wine
Poured on its waters, till the contented brine
Gave forth new odors, and a pleasant scent
Of rare perfume; and haggard men, all spent
With long, sharp sickness, drank in life anew,
When the rich sea-breeze through their lattice blew
Bacchos! who tramplest Care with thy soft feet,
Oh, hither turn thy tigers, strong and fleet,
     And light our happy isles
     With the radiance of thy smiles!
Come, with thy hair dewy with wine, and meet
Those who, for thee, have trod the weary miles.

IV.

Come to our ceremony! Lo, we rear
An altar of green turf, the sea-beach near,
And garland it with vine-shoots, and the leaf
Of glossy ivy. Come! and chase all grief
Far from us! Lo! upon the turf we pour
Full cups of wine, till all along the shore
Eddies the luscious odor. See! a mist
Is rising from the wine-stained turf—(Ah, hist!—
Alas! 'twas not his cry!)—Come with thy train
Of riotous Satyrs, pouring forth a strain
Of utmost shrillness on the noisy pipe.
Come, with thine eye and lip of beauty ripe
And wondrous rare, and let us hear thy wheels
Rolling along the hills, while twilight steals
Quietly up, and dusky, sober Night
Is hindered from her star-track by the light
Of thy wild tigers' eyes! Cross the calm sea
With all thy mad and merry company!
     The stars shall wax and wane,
     And ere day comes again,
We'll wander over hill and vale with thee,
Sending afar a loudly joyous strain.

1829.

"Hear, 'Aphrodite! Hear our rustic song!
Thalassia, hear! for unto thee belong
All pleasant offerings; ring-doves coo to thee,
While they entwine their arch'd necks lovingly."

TO 'APHRODĪTĒ.

I.

Oh, thou most lovely and most beautiful!—
Wherever cooingly thy white doves lull
Thy bright eyes to soft slumber; whether on
The truant south-wind floating, or if gone
To some still cloud in dreamy sleep that swings,
And there reclining, while its snowy wings
Blush into crimson: whether thy delicate wheels,
Over green sward that scarce the pressure feels,
Brush the bright dewdrops from the bending grass,
Leaving the poor, green blades to look, alas!
With dim eyes at the moon,—(Ah! so dost thou
Dim other eyes and brighter!)—whether now
Thou floatest over the sea, while each white wing
Of thy fair doves is wet, and sea-maids bring
Sweet odours for thee,—(Ah! how foolish they!
    They have not felt thy smart,
They know not, while in ocean-waves they play,
    How cruel and strong thou art!)

II.

Hear, 'Aphrodite!   Hear our rustic song!
Thalassia, hear! for unto thee belong

All pleasant offerings; ring-doves coo to thee,
While they entwine their arch'd necks lovingly,
Among the murmuring leaves; thine are all sounds
Of pleasure on earth; and where abounds
Most happiness, for thee we surely look.—
In the dusk depths of some leaf-shaded nook
Thou hidest frequently, where soft winds wave
Thy sunny curls, and cool airs fondly lave
Thy radiant brow, and ruffle the delicate wings
Of thy tired doves; where his quaint love-tale sings,
With small, bright eyes, some little, strange, sweet bird,
In notes that never but by thee are heard.—
In some such spot dreaming thou liest now,
    And with half-open eye,
Drinkest in beauty.   Fairest of heaven, do thou
    Hear kindly our faint cry!

III.

Doris! from whom all things upon this earth
Take light and life; for whom even laughing Mirth
Doubles his glee; thou, whom the joyous bird
Continually sings; whose name is heard
In every pleasant noise; at whose warm glance
All things look brighter; for whom wine doth dance
More merrily within the agate vase,
To meet thy lip; glimpsing at whose sweet face,
Joy leaps on faster, with a clearer laugh,

And Sorrow flings into the sea his staff,
And tossing back the hair from his dim eyes,
Looks up again to long-forgotten skies;
While Avarice forgets to count his gold,
And even offers thee his wealth untold,
Dear as his heart's blood. Thou to whose high might
    All things are glad to bow,
Come unto us, and with thy looks of light,
    Bless and console us now!

IV.

Hear us, 'Ourania! Thou whom all obey!
At whose sweet will rough Satyrs leave their play,
And gather wild flowers to adorn the hair
Of the young nymphs, and nuts and berries bear
To those they fancy most. Paphia, to whom
They leap in awkward mood through the dusk gloom
Of darkening oak-trees, or at sunny noon
Play unto thee, on their rude pipes, a tune
Of wondrous languishment! Thou, whose great power
Brings up young sea-maids from each ocean-bower,
With many an idle song to sing to thee,
And bright locks floating mist-like on the sea,
And glancing eyes, as if in distant caves
They spied their lovers,—(so along blue waves
Small bubbles flit, mocking the genial sun;)—

Let cares no more oppress
Thy servitors! but, ere our feast is done,
   Our new loves kindly bless!

V.

Oh, thou who once didst weep, and with sad tears
Bedew the pitying woods! by those great fears
That haunted thee when young Adonis lay
With dark eyes drowned in death;—by that dull day
That saw him, wounded, fall, with many a moan,
On the dead leaves, and sadly and alone
Breathe out his life;—deign thou to look upon
All maidens who for too great love grow wan
And pity them! Come to us when Night brings
Her first faint stars; and let us hear the wings
Of thy most beautiful and bright-eyed doves,
Fanning the breathless air. Let all the Loves
Fly round thy chariot, with sweet, low songs
Murmuring upon their lips. Come! each maid longs
For thy fair presence, Goddess of true Love!
   Float through the odorous air,
And, as thy light wheels roll, from us remove
   Sadness and love-sick care.

VI.

Lo! we have many kinds of incense here,
To burn to thee; wine as the sunshine clear,
Fit for young Bacchos; flowers we have here, too,

Gathered by star-light, when the morning-dew
Was fresh upon them; myrtle-wreaths we bear,
To place upon thy bright, luxuriant hair,
And shade thy temples. 'Tis the proper time
For all fair beauty. Thou, who lovest the clime
Of our dear isle, where roses bud and blow
With honey in their bosoms, and a glow
Like thine own cheek, lifting their modest heads,
To be refreshed with the transparent beads
Of diamond dew, paling the young moon's rays,—
Our altars burn for thee, and on the blaze
We pour rich incense from great golden vases.
    Queen Cypria! hear our words,
And hither urge, circled with all the Graces,
    Thy team of snow-winged birds!

1829.

No. 6.

TO APOLLŌN.

I.

Bright-haired Apollon! Thou that ever art
A blessing to the world! whose generous heart
Aye overflows with love and light and life!
Thou, at whose glance all things on earth are rife
With happiness! to whom, in early Spring,

23

Flowers lift their heads, whether they laughing cling
To the steep mountain's side, or in the vale
Timidly nestle! Thou, to whom the pale
Chill, weary Earth looks up, when Winter flees,
With patient gaze, and the storm-shattered trees
Put forth fresh leaves, and drink deep draughts of light,
Poured from thy brilliant orb! Thou in whose bright,
Coruscant rays, the eagle feeds his eye
With flashing fire, and far, far up on high
Screams out his haughty joy! By all the names
And the high titles that thy Godhead claims,—
Phoibos, or Clarios, golden-haired Apollo,
Cunthios, or Puthios,—cease for a time to follow
    The fleeing Night, and hear
    Our hymn to thee, and smilingly draw near!

II.

Most exquisite poet! Thou, whose great heart's swell
Pours itself out on mountain, lawn, and dell!
Thou who dost touch them with thy golden feet,
And make them for the Painter's use complete;
Inspired by whom the Poet's eyes perceive
Great beauty everywhere,—in the slow heave
Of the unquiet sea, or in the roar
Of its resounding waters,—on the shore
Of pleasant streams,—in the dark, jagged rift
Of savage mountains, where the black clouds drift,

Flushed with swift lightning,—on the broad, dark brow
Of silent Night, that solemnly and slow
Walks up the sky. Oh, thou, whose influence
Tinges all things with beauty, makes each sense
Double delight, and clothes with a delicate grace
All that is young and fair; while all the base
Flits far, like darkness!—thou that art in truth
Incarnate lordliness, hear! while our youth

    With earnest yearning cry;
    Answer our hymn, and come to us, Most high!

III.

In quaint disguise, with wóndrous grace and fire,
Often thou makest, on thy golden lyre,
Exquisite music, on smooth, sunny glades,
Where on the greensward dance the village maids,
Their hair adorned with wild-flowers, or a wreath
Of thine own laurel; while, reclined beneath
Some ancient oak, thou smilest at these elves,
As though thou wert all human like themselves.
Sometimes thou playest in the darkening wood,
While Fauns glide forth, in dance grotesque and rude,
Flitting among the trees with awkward leap,
Like their god, Pan; and from fir-thickets deep
Come up the Satyrs, joining the mad crew,
And capering for thy pleasure. From each yew,
And beech, and oak, the wood-nymphs shyly peep,

To see the revelry; and from its sleep
The merry laughter wakes the startled wood,
And music cheers its dusk, deep solitude.
      Oh, come, and let the sound
      Of thy sweet lyre eddy our isle around!

IV.

Great Seer and Prophet! Thou that teachest men
The deepest-hidden lore, and from his den
Dost pluck the Future, so that he floats by
In visible shape, apparent to the eye,
But robed with visions: thou, in whose high power
Are health and sickness: thou who oft dost shower
Great plagues on impious nations, with hot breath
Withering their souls, and raining sudden death
Like fiery mist among them; or, again,
Like the sweet breeze after a summer rain,
That thrills the earth like love, thou sendest out
Health, like a lovely child, that goes about,
With soft, white feet, among the sick and weak,
Kissing with rosy lip each poor pale cheek,
Shaking perfume from its white wings, and through
The shriveled heart stirring the blood, anew
To fill the abandoned veins. Oh, thou, whose name
Is hymned by all, let us, too, dare to claim
      Thy holy presence here!
      Hear us, bright God, and lend a gracious ear!

V.

Hear us! Thou master of the springing bow,
Who lovest in the gloomy woods to throw
Thine arrows to the mark, like the keen flight
Of those that fill the universe with light,
From the sun's quiver shot! From whom grim bears
And lordly lions flee, timid as hares,
To hide among safe mountains! Thou, whose cry
Sounds in the autumn-woods, where whirl and fly
The brown dry leaves,—when with his riotous train
Bacchos is on the hills, and on the plain
Full-armed Demeter; when upon the sea
The brine-gods blow their shells, and laughingly
The broad world rings with glee. Then thy clear voice
Stills into silence every truant noise,
Pealing with utmost sweetness on the hills,
And in the echoes of the dancing rills,
Over the sea and on the sounding plain,
And eddying air, until all voices wane
        Before its influence:
        Draw near, great God, before the day goes hence!

VI.

By that most fatal day, when with a cry
Young Huakinthos fell, and his dark eye
Was dimmed with blood,—when, dying, on a bed

Of his own flowers he laid his wounded head,
Breathing great sighs; by those heart-cherished eyes
Of long-loved Huakinthos, by the sighs
That then, oh, young Apollon, thou didst pour
On every gloomy hill and desolate shore,
Weeping away thy soul, and making dull
Thine eyes with eclipse, till the chilled earth was full
Of sad forebodings, for thy radiance dimmed;
Prayers by pale priests in many a fane were hymned
To the pale-eyed Sun; the frightened Satyrs strayed
Long in the dark woods, and then to the chill glade
Came to lament that thou wast still unkind;
Artemis wept for love, and pained and pined
For light and life: by that most fearful grief,
Oh! bright Apollon, hear, and grant relief

To us who cry to thee!
And let us, ere we die, thy glory see!

1829.

No. 7.

TO ARTEMIS.

I.

Most graceful Goddess! whether now thy feet
Pursue the dun deer to their deep retreat
In the heart of some old wood, or on the side

Of some high mountain; where, most eager-eyed,
Thou glidest on the chase, with bended bow,
And arrow at the string, a wondrous glow
Of exquisite beauty on thy cheek, and feet
White as the silver moon, graceful and fleet
As her soft rays,—with quiver at thy back
Rattling to all thy steppings. If some track
In far-off Thessaly thou followest up,
Brushing the dew from many a flower's full cup,
With head bent forward, harking to the bay
Of thy good hounds, while in the deep woods they,
Strong-limbed and swift, leap on with eager bounds,
And from far hills their long, deep note resounds,
Thy sweetest music: Orthia, hear our cry,
And let us worship thee, while far and high
Climbs up thy brother,—while his light falls full
Upon the earth,—for when the night-winds lull

    The world to sleep, then to the lightless sky
Delia must glide, with robes of silver dew

      And sunward eye!

II.

Perhaps thou hiest to some shady spot
Among broad trees, while frightened beasts hear not
The clamor of thy hounds; there, dropping down
Upon green grass and leaves all sere and brown,
Thou pillowest thy delicate head upon

Some gnarled and moss-robed root, where soft winds run
Riot about thee, and thy fair Nymphs point
Thy death-winged arrows, or thy hair anoint
With Lydian odors; and thy strong hounds lie
Lazily on the ground, and watch thine eye,
And watch thine arrows, while thou hast a dream.
Perhaps in some deep-bosomed, shaded stream
Thou bathest now, where even the loving Sun
Catches no glimpse of thee; where shadows on
The waters dusk collect, and make it cool,
Like the wind-chilled wide sea, or some clear pool
Deep in a cavern; hanging branches dip
Their ringlets in the stream, or slowly drip
With tear-drops of clear dew: before no eyes
But those of flitting wind-gods, each nymph hies

    Into the deep, cool, rippling stream, and there
Thou pillowest thyself upon its breast,

      Queen Cynthia, the Fair.

III.

By all thine hours of pleasure!—when thou wast
Upon tall Latmos, moveless, tranced, and lost
In boundless pleasure, ever gazing on
Thy bright-eyed youngster; when the absent Sun
Was lighting remote seas, or at mid-noon
Careering through the sky! By every tune
And voice of joy that thrilled about the chords

Of thy great heart, when on it fell his words,
In that cool, shady nook, where thou hadst brought
And placed Endumion;—where fair hands had taught
All beauty to shine forth; where thy young maids
Had brought rare shells for him, and from the glades
All starry flowers, with precious stones, and gems
Of utmost beauty, pearly diadems
Of ancient sea-gods: birds were there, that sang
And carolled ever; living waters rang
Their changes at all times, to soothe the soul
Of thy Endumion; pleasant breezes stole
With light feet through the nook, that they might kiss
His dewy lips. Ah! by those hours of bliss,
    Worth a whole life in heaven, come to us, fair
And beautiful Aricia! Take us under
    Thy gentle care.

1829.

No. 8.

TO ARES.

I.

Great War-God! mighty Ares! Hear our hymn,
Sung to thee in the wood-recesses dim
Of dusky Caria, near the Icarian wave!—

When war's red storms in lurid fury rave,
And the fierce billows of his hungry tide
Over the groaning land sweep far and wide;—
When his thick legions, clad in gleaming steel,
And bristling thick with javelins, madly reel
In desperate conflict;—when the mighty roar
Peals upward, shaking heaven's great golden floor,
Even as the tumult of the maddened sea
Shakes granite towers;—when Fear, and Agony,
And Desperation, riot, hand-in-hand,
And Fire and Famine waste the lean, lank land:—
Then thou, rejoicing, ragest through the field;
Like mountain-thunder clangs thy brazen shield;
Thy falchion, like the lightning, flashes far;
The frightened Earth, under thy sounding car,
(Whirled swiftly by thy brazen-footed steeds,
Flight and mad Terror), shuddering, quakes and shivers;
    And ever, as the war's red surge recedes,
Brooks swelled with blood run downward to red rivers.

II.

Turn thy wild coursers from our lovely land!
Let not their hoofs trample our golden strand!
Shake not thy spear above our fruitful hills,
Nor turn to blood the waters of our rills!
Crush not our flowers with thy remorseless wheels,
Nor let our grain be trod with armed heels,

That the poor starve! Let not thy sister ride,
With Pestilence and Famine, by thy side;
But come with Aphrodite in thy arms
Enfolded, radiant with a thousand charms,—
Her lovely head held on thy massive chest,
Her sweet eyes soothing into placid rest
Thy fiery passions; while her doves glide through
The sparkling atmosphere. Bring with thee, too,
Thy lovely children, at their mother's side;—
Eros, whose form expands, and wings grow wide,
When his sweet brother, Anteros, is near,
The God of tenderest love, and faith sincere;—

    With fair Harmonia clinging to thy neck,
And mingling music with her glad caresses;

    While the young Charities flit round, and deck
With dew-enjewelled flowers thy loved one's golden tresses,

III.

Let thy harsh wheels roll through Abarimon,
Where Mount Imaus glitters in the sun,
Throned like a king, in solitary state:
Make there more rugged and more desolate
The frozen Scythian wildernesses; grind
To dust the Indian rocks, and like the wind
Drive thy fleet coursers through the Median plains,
And over Bactria's barbarous domains;
But spare the isles of our beloved Greece,
And leave them sleeping tranquilly in peace.

Here, under an old, stately, branching oak,
Thine altar sendeth to the clouds its smoke,
Whereon the wolf and hungry vulture bleed,
The magpie, and the bold and generous steed.
We bow in adoration at thy shrine,
Dark-bearded God, majestic and divine!
Our incense, burning, loads the eddying air,
And Kuthereia joins us in our prayer.

    Wilt thou not listen kindly to the strain
Which now around our vine-clad hills is pealing?

    For when did Beauty ever sue in vain,
Even in his sternest mood meekly to Valor kneeling?

No. 9.

TO PALLAS.

I.

Hear, blue-eyed Pallas! Eagerly we call,
Entreating thee to our glad festival,
Held in the sunny morning of the year,
On this our rosy isle, to thee most dear.
Thine altar, builded by young maidens' hands,
Near the Carpathian's sparkling water stands,

Upon the slant and sunny Rhodian shore,
Gracing the green lawn's undulating floor,
Walled in with trees, which, sweeping wide around,
Rampart the precincts of the holy ground.
Myriads of roses, flushing full in bloom,
Send to far Caria surge of rich perfume,
Like the glad incense of our prayer, which floats
Up to the trembling stars. The ringing notes
Of silver flutes roll through the echoing woods,
Startling the Fauns in their shy solitudes.
A hundred boys, each fairer than a girl,
Over the greensward, clad in armor, whirl
In thy wild mystic dance. A hundred maids,
In white and gold, come from the dusky glades,—
The loveliest of our beauty-blessed isle,—
Their small white feet gleaming like stars, that smile
In the dark azure of a moonless night.
They bear thy robe of pure and stainless white,
    Sleeveless, embroidered richly with fine gold,
    Whereon thy deeds are told,
    Those, chiefly, done of old,
When, blazing in the van, thou didst the Giants fight.

II.

Brain-born of Zeus! Thou who dost give to men
Knowledge and wisdom; and hast brought again
Science and art, in renovated youth,

And taught fair Greece to love and seek the truth;
Thou to whom artist and artificer,
Fearing thy potent anger to incur,
Bend down beseechingly, and pray for aid
In all the cunning mysteries of their trade;
Inspired by thee, young men, immersed in cells,
Drink deep of learning, at Time's ancient wells,
Forget that Beauty's starry eyes still shine,
And love Athene only, the Divine:
Old gray-haired sages pore on antique scrolls,
And feed with wisdom's oil their burning souls,
Inspired by thee, the prophet sees afar
The signs of peace, the portents of grim war;
Foretells the strange and wayward destinies
Of nations and of men, and when the skies
With genial rains will bless the husbandman,
Or vex the earth with hail. Thy favor can
The life of those well loved by thee prolong,
And make hoar Eld youthful again and strong.
Oh, come to us! while glittering with dew
Young Day still crimsons the horizon's blue!

  Come, Parthenos! to thy beloved home,
   Nor longer idly roam,
   Where hungry oceans foam,
Round barbarous continents and islands new.

III.

Oh, come not to us, clad in armor bright,
Intolerable unto mortal sight,
With flashing spear, and helm of blazing gold,
Crested with griffin-guarded sphynx! nor hold
Thine aegis, blazing with Medusa's eye,
Wreathed with live serpents! Not in warlike guise,
As when against the Giants thou didst march,
With strong tread shaking earth and the sky's great arch,
Terrific in thy panoply of war,
Jove's lightning in thy right hand flashing far;
Till, struck with fear and overpowering dread,
Heaven's baffled adversaries howling fled!
Come in thy garb of peace, with kindly smile,
Breathing new beauty on thy flowery isle;
With mystic veil over thy dazzling brow,
And soft feet, whiter than the mountain-snow!
Come to us over the exulting sea,
From thy Tegaean shrine in Arcady;
Thy sacred dragon gliding o'er the waves,
While nymphs, emerging from deep ocean-caves,
Floating like stars upon the misty spray,
Carol around thee many a pleasant lay;
And grim Poseidon, smiling at the strain,
Gives thee glad welcome to his vast domain;

And Aiolos bears incense from the shores,
Where the mad Ganges roars,
And his great torrent pours
I' th' Indian sea, and all the trees rich odors rain.

IV.

Thou who the daring Argonauts didst guide
Over the stormy sea's rebellious tide;
By Lemnos and by sunny Samothrace,
(Fair isles, that sit the waves with swan-like grace,)
By Troas and the dark Symplegades;
And send them, with a favorable breeze,
Through the wide Euxine into Colchis; hear!
Oh, Virgin Goddess! and come smiling near,
While here we wait upon the silver sands,
And stretch imploringly our suppliant hands!
Then shall our maidens, of long summer eves,
Embowered among the overshading leaves,
(While, taught of thee, their sweet task they fulfill,
Plying the distaff with a curious skill,)
Tell of the time, when, brighter than a star,
Approaching on the azure sea afar,
Thou didst our humble ceremonies bless,
And smile upon their budding loveliness,—
When new flowers sprang in every sunny vale,
New odors loaded every pleasant gale,
And whiter corn, and richer wine and oil,
Thenceforward paid the husbandman's glad toil;

And blander breezes, and serener skies
Thereafter blessed the isle. Oh, good and wise!
    Oh, radiant Goddess! Shall this sacred day
    Glide mournfully away,
    Fading to evening gray,
And thou not deign to glad our anxious, longing eyes?

                          1845.

No. 10.

TO HERMĒS.

I.

Hear, white-winged Messenger! If thy swift feet
Loiter within Heaven's starry walls, where meet
The Gods, their nectar daintily to sip
At indolent leisure; where thy beardless lip
Utters such eloquence, that thine old foe,
Imperial Here, doth her hate forego,
And hang entranced on thy sweet accents, while
Cypria rewards thee with inviting smile,
And wise Athene's cup stands waiting by,
Till thou hast ended;—whether, near the sky,
Among the palpitating stars thou soarest,
Or foldest thy bright pinions in some forest

That crowns an Asian mountain;—if thy wings
Fan the broad sea, where sultry Afric flings
His hot breath on the waters, by the shore
Of Araby the blest; or in the roar
Of crashing Northern ice:—oh, turn, and urge,
Thy winged course to us! Leave the rough surge,
Or icy mountain-height, or city proud,
Or haughty temple, or dim wood, down-bowed
    With weakening age,
And come to us, thou young and mighty sage!

II.

Thou who invisibly dost ever stand
Near each high orator, and hand-in-hand
With golden-robed Apollon, touch the tongue
Of the rapt poet; on whom men have hung,
Strangely enchanted, when, in dark disguise,
Thou hast descended from cloud-curtained skies,
And lifted up thy voice to teach bold men
Thy world-arousing art! Oh thou, that when
The ocean was untracked, didst teach them send
Great ships upon it! Thou who dost extend,
In storm or calm, protection to the hopes
Of the fair merchant! Thou, that on the slopes
Of Mount Kullene first mad'st sound the lyre
And the delicious harp,—with childish fire
And magical beauty playing, in dark caves

Marvellous tunes, unlike the ruder staves
That Pan had uttered; while each wondering Nymph
Came out from tree and mountain, and the lymph
Of mountain-stream, to drink each echoing note
That over the entranced woods did float,

    With fine clear tone,
Like silver trumpets on a still lake blown.

III.

Thou matchless Artist! Thou, whose wondrous skill,
In ages past the earth's wide bounds did fill
With every usefulness! Thou, who dost teach
Quick-witted thieves the miser's gold to reach,
And rob him of his sleep for many a night,
Getting thee curses! Mischievous, mad sprite!
Young Rogue-God Hermes! always glad to cheat
All Gods and men;—with mute and noiseless feet
Going in search of mischief; now to steal
The spear of Ares, now to clog the wheel
Of young Apollon's car, that it may crawl
Most slowly upwards! Thou, whom wrestlers call,
Whether they strive upon the level green
At dewy nightfall, under the dim screen
Of ancient oaks, or at the sacred games,
In fiercer contest! Thou, whom each then names
In half-thought prayer, when the quick breath is drawn

For the last struggle! Thou, whom, on the lawn,
The victor praises, and ascribes to thee
His fresh-reaped honors! Let us ever be
    Under thy care,
And hear, oh hear, our solemn, earnest prayer.

1829.

No. 11.

TO FLORA.

I.

Hear, lovely Chloris, while we sing to thee!
Thou restest now beneath some shady tree,
Near a swift brook, upon a mossy root;
All other winds with deep delight are mute,
While Euros frolics with thy flowing hair,
A thousand odors floating on the air,
And rippling softly through the dewy green
Of the thick leaves, that murmuringly screen
Thy snowy forehead. Struggling through their mass,
The quivering sunlight snows upon the grass
In golden flakes. Round thee a thousand flowers,
Still glittering with the tears of Spring's light showers,

Offer the incense of their glad perfume
To thee, who makest them to bud and bloom,
With thy kind smile and influence divine.
Thine arms around young Zephuros entwine,
And his 'round thee. With roses garlanded,
On his white shoulder rests thy lovely head;
    Thy deep eyes gaze in his,
Radiant with mute, unutterable bliss,
    And, happy there,
     Oh, lovely, young, enamored pair,
Your rosy lips oft meet in many a long, warm kiss!

II.

Now the young Spring rejoices, and is glad,
 In her new robes of starry blossoms clad;
The happy earth smiles like an innocent bride,
That sitteth, blushing, by her husband's side;
The bird her nest with earnest patience weaves,
And sings, delighted, hidden in the leaves;
From their high homes in cavernous old trees,
The busy legions of industrious bees
Drink nectar at each flower's enamelled brim,
Breathing in murmured music their glad hymn;
The Nereids come from their deep ocean-caves,
Deserting for a time the saddened waves;
The Druads from the dusky solitudes,

Of venerable and majestic woods;
The Naiads from deep beech-embowered lakes;
The Oreads from where hoarse Thunder shakes
The iron mountains;—wandering through cool glades,
And blushing lawns, when first the darkness fades,
    Before the crimsoning morn,
And ere the young Day's sapphire tints are gone,
    In glad haste all,
    Their lovers to enwreathe withal,
Gather the fresh-blown flowers, gemmed with the tears of
        Dawn.

III.

Come, gentle Queen! we spill to thee no blood;
Thine altar stands where the gray, ancient wood,
Now green with leaves, and fresh with April rains,
In stately circle sweeping round, contains,
Embowered like a hill-environed dell,
A quiet lawn, whose undulations swell
Green as the sea-waves. Near a bubbling spring,
Whose waters, sparkling downward, lightly ring
On the small pebbles—round whose grassy lip
The birds and bees its crystal waters sip—
Thine altar stands, of shrubs and flowering vines,
Where rose with lily and carnation twines.
We burn to thee no incense. These fresh blooms,
Breathe on the air more exquisite perfumes,
Than all that press the overladen wind

44

That seaward floats from Araby to Ind.

No priests are here prepared for sacrifice,

But fair young girls, with mischievous, bright eyes,

    With white flowers garlanded,

And by their young, delighted lovers led,

    With frequent kisses,

      And fond and innocent caresses,

To honor thee, the victim and the priest instead.

                         1845.

No. 12.

TO HUPNOS.

I.

Kind Comforter of all the weary Gods,

With drooping eyelids, head that ever nods!

Thou silent soother, that with all thy train

Of empty dreams, dim tenants of the brain,

Vague as the wind, dost sleep in thy dark cave,

At whose mouth sluggishly white poppies wave,

In the light airs that saunter by thy bed,—

Thine only throne, with darkness tenanted,

And curtains black as are the eyes of Night!—

Thou, who dost sleep, when wanes the reluctant light,

Deep in lone forests, where gray Evening hides,

Trembling at sight of the sun; and Shadow glides

45

Through silent tree-tops: or, if, half-awake,
Thou dozest on the margin of some lake,
Land-locked, and still as the mute, cloudless sky;
While thy quaint Dreams, wayward and wanton, fly,
With mischievous pranks, fantastic tricks, mad mirth,
    About the sluggard, Earth:
Oh, come, and hear the hymn that we are chanting,—
Here, where the shivered starlight through thick leaves is
    slanting!

II.

Thou lover of the banks of idle streams,
Shadowed by broad old oaks, with gleams scattered
From moon and stars upon them;—of the ocean,
When its great bosom throbs with no emotion,
But the round moon hangs out her lamp, to pour
A sparkling glory on its level floor!
Thou, that reclinest on the moist, warm sands,
While winds come dancing from far southern lands,
With dreams upon their backs, and wings that reek
And drip with odors; or upon a peak
Of cloud, that, like a hill of chrysolite,
Leans on the western sky, when the bland night
Comes late in summer; or beneath the sea,
Scarce conscious of the dim monotony
Of the great waves, here murmuring like the wings
Of swarming dreams, while the huge ocean swings

His bulk above thy listless, heavy head!

    (As, chained upon his bed,

A conquered Titan, with unconscious motion,—

Even so respiring swings the mute and sleeping ocean.)

III.

Thou who dost bless sad mourners with thy touch,

And make sharp Agony relax his clutch

Upon the bleeding fibres of the heart,

Pale Disappointment no more mope apart,

And Sorrow dry her tears, and cease to weep

Her life away, gaining new cheer in sleep!

Thou who dost bless the birds, at evening gray,

When, tired of singing all the summer day,

They, longing, watch to see the evening star,—

Thy herald,—on the sky's blue slope! Where are

Thy flocks of flitting dreams, dear God, by whom

All noise is most abhorred? Come to this gloom,

So cool, so fresh, where nought the silence stirs,

Except the murmur of the dreaming firs!

Touch our tired eyes! Make the dusk shades more dense!

Ah! thou hast come! We feel thine influence,

Forget our hymn, and sink in sleep away;

    And so, till new-born Day

Climbs high in heaven, with fire-steeds swiftly leaping,

Here we'll recline, beneath the vine-leaves calmly sleeping.

1830.

LATONA.

There was a sudden stir,
Ages ago, on the Ægean Sea.
With a loud cry, as of great agony,
The blue deep parted, and the angry roar
Of a great earthquake echoed round the shore;
The tortured waters, trembling, stood aghast;
Delos emerged, and anchored firm and fast
Among the Cyclades, lay calm and still.
In one brief moment, valley, plain and hill
Were carpeted with verdure, and great trees
Sprung to full stature, shaking in the breeze
Their limbs and leaves; and fruits, and buds, and flowers
Longed for the sunshine and the summer showers.
Pursued by Here, poor Latona had
Till then been wandering, terrified and sad,
Round the great earth, and through the weltering seas,
Praying for mercy on long-bended knees,
But still denied. Many a weary day,
Above the shaggy hills, where, groaning, lay

Enceladus and Typhon, she had roamed,
And over volcanoes where lava foamed;
And sometimes in dark forests she had hid,
Where the lithe serpent through the long grass slid,
Over gray weeds and tiger-trampled flowers;
Where the grim lion couched in tangled bowers,
And the fierce panther, proud of his dappled skin,
Startled the woods with his deep, moaning din.
All things were there to terrify the soul:—
The hedgehog that across her path did roll,
Gray eagles, fanged like pards, old vultures bald,
Fierce hawks, and restless owls, whose hoot appalled;
Red scorpions, lurking under mossy stones,
And here and there great piles of rotting bones
Of the first men who won renown in wars;
Brass heads of arrows, javelins, scimetars,
Old crescent shield, and edgeless battle-axe;
Large yellow skulls, with wide and gaping cracks,
Too old and dry for worms to harbor in,—
Only the useless spider there did spin
His treacherous web.

        Then would she stop, and lay
Her weary head among dead leaves and pray
That she might die,—and fainting thus remain,
Pulseless, till thou, O Zeus! wouldst rise, and rain

Thy light upon her eyelids. Then the tide
Of life once more through her cold heart would glide,
Her soul grow strong, and once more fit to cope
With all her fate, and many a cheerful hope
Glow in her heart; then, O King Zeus! wouldst thou
With the bright terrors of thy frowning brow,
Scare every hateful creature far away.
Then would she rise, fairer than rosy Day,
And through the tiger-peopled solitudes,
And odorous brakes, and panther-guarded woods
Journey, until she reached the curving edge
Of the blue sea; and there, on some high ledge
Of porphyritic rock, sit long, and look
Into thine eye, nor fear that from some nook
The hideous shapes that haunted her would meet
Her startled eyes.

       One day she cooled her feet
On a long, narrow beach. The encroaching brine
Had marked, as with an endless serpent-spine,
The hard, smooth sand with a long line of shells,
Like those the Nereids gather, in deep cells
Of the sea, for Thetis: such they pile around
The feet of cross old Nereus, having found
That this propitiates him; such they bring
To slippery Proteus as an offering,
When they would have him tell their destiny,
And what young God their first love is to be.

And there Latona paced along the sands,
Dreaming of journeys into unknown lands,
And persecutions to be suffered yet:
And when some wave, less shy than others, wet
Her rosy feet, she tingled as when Thou
Didst first thy lips press on her blushing brow.
Still she paced on over the firm, cool sand,
And the heaped shells, and, once or twice, would stand
And let her long, bright, golden tresses float
Over the waters. Lo! the threatening note
Of the fierce, hissing Dragon strikes her ear!
Startled, she shivers with a horrid fear,
And, mad with terror and insáne despair,
Flees to the sea, and seeks destruction there.
But thy great Brother met her as she fell
Into the waves, and gave her power to dwell
Beneath the waters, like a Naiad, born
Within the sound of Triton's mellow shell,
That stills the waves. Then wandered she forlorn
Through many wonders:—coral-raftered caves,
Sunk far below the roar of clamorous waves;
Sea-flowers like masses of soft golden hair
Or misty silk; great shells, and fleshless spine
Of old Behemoth; flasks of hoarded wine,
Among the timbers of old, shattered ships;
Goblets of gold, that had not touched the lips
Of men a thousand years.

                        At length she lay,
Despairing, down, to weep her life away
On the sea's floor, alone;—and then it was
Thy mighty voice, the Deities that awes,
Lifted to light under fair Grecian skies
That lovely Cycladean Paradise,
And placed Latona there, when fast asleep,
With parted lips, and respiration deep,
And all unconscious. When, refreshed, she woke,
She lay beneath a tall, wide-branching oak,
Majestic, king-like,—from whose depths peeped out
All those shy birds whose instinct is to doubt
And fear mankind. Doves, with soft, patient eyes,
Did earnestly artistic nests devise,
Busy as bees under the sheltering leaves;
Thrushes that love to house beneath mossed eaves;
Merles, brought from the far Azores, with their clear,
Mellow, and fluty note;—the chaffinch, dear
To the rude Thuringian, for its mazy trills;
The mountain-finch, from Shetland's rugged hills,
With its brown eyes, and neck of velvet-black;
The sweet canary, yearning to flit back
To his own isles;—the small gold-crested wren,
Uttering its hurried trill of terror, when
Aught hostile came anear its elegant nest,
And pale-brown eggs;—the skylark, with his breast
Wet with the morning dew, who never sings

Upon the ground, but whose fine music rings
High in the heavens;—the golden oriole,
That mimics the rude flourishes which roll
From braying trumpets, with his flute-like notes;
Affectionate redstarts, who, with mellow throats,
First hail the dawn;—song-throstles, bold and fond
From Smyrna and from ancient Trebizond,
That sing in lofty tree-tops, at still noon,
A musical and melancholy tune;
The happy bullfinch, with his modest song,
Low, soft, and sweet,—rose-ouzels, and a throng
Of mountain linnets from the Orkney Isles,
And warbling ortolons, from where the smiles
Of the warm sun ripen the grapes of France;
The frisking white-throat, with his antic dance,
That sings at sultry summer-noon, and chases
The small aphides through the tangled mazes
Of rose and honeysuckle;—black-caps, nesting
In the white thorn; who, while the world is resting,
At midnight, wake with full, sweet melodies,
Wild, deep and loud, the sleep-enchanted bees;
Blue-throated robins, bred near northern seas;
And pied fly-catchers, nesting in old trees;
And, last of all, the peerless nightingale.—
Cicadas sang, hid in the velvet grass;
Bees all around did their rich store amass,
Or clung together on a swinging bough,

In tangled swarms;—above her pale, fair brow
Hung nests of callow songsters; and so nigh
That she could touch it, lay, with lively eye,
A small, gray lizard; such do notice give
When serpents glide; and in all lands they live,
Even by the good-will of the rudest hind.
Close to her feet an antelope reclined,
Graceful, large-eyed, white as the stainless fleece
Of snow upon the topmost Pyrenees,
And cropped the young buds of the sheltering trees
From the drooping limbs. In the deep, sombre woods
No voice stirred; nor in these sweet solitudes
Did aught disturb the birds, except the hymn
Sung by the fountain, from whose grassy brim
Its liquid light, in thin, clear, sparkling jets,
Rained ever on the thirsty violets;
The hum of leaves that whispered overhead,
The brook that sang along its pebbly bed,
The water-fall deep in the forest hid,
And the slight murmur of the waves, that slid
As softly up the firm, unyielding sand,
As gentle children, clasping hand and hand,
In the sick chamber of a mother grieve,
And glide on tiptoe.—

                Here, O Zeus, one eve,
When thou didst shine high in the darkling west,
And bathe Night's glossy hair and ebon breast,

And gentle eyes with brightness,—while the Earth
Sent up soft mists to thee, thy maid gave birth
To bright Apollo, and his sister fair,
The ivory-footed Huntress;—such a pair,
Tall-statured, beautiful, as now they sit
On golden thrones, where, on Olympus met,
The austere Senate of the immortal Gods
Obeys and trembles if the Thunderer nods.—
And when the radiant wings of morning stirred
The darkness in the East, Latona heard,
Faint and far-off, the well-remembered hiss
Of the great dragon. Bitter agonies
Shot through her soul, and she had swiftly fled,
And tried again old Ocean's friendly bed,
Had not Apollo, young, sun-bright Apollo,
Restrained her from the dark and perilous hollow,
And asked what meant the noise.

              "It is," she said,
"The monster Python, a great dragon, bred
After the Deluge, in the stagnant mud,
And thirsting for thy mother's innocent blood,
Sent by great Here, Heaven's vindictive Queen,
To slay us all."

              Upon the dewy green
Lay ready to the hand a nervous bow
And heavy arrows, eagle-winged, which thou,
Oh, Zeus! hadst placed within Apollo's reach.

These grasping, the young God stood in the breach
Of circling trees, with eye that fiercely glanced,
Nostril expanded, lip pressed, foot advanced,
And arrow at the string; when, lo! the coil
Of the great dragon came, with sinuous toil,
And vast gyrations, crushing down the branches,
With noise as when a hungry tiger cranches
Huge bones; and then Apollo drew the bow
Full at the eye, nor ended with one blow;
Dart after dart sped from the twanging string,
All at the eye: until, a lifeless thing,
The dragon lay.—

   Thus the young Sun-God slew
The scaly monster; and then dragged and threw,
(So strong he was), the carcass in the sea,
Where the great sharks feasted voraciously,
Lashing the water into bloody foam
In their fierce fights.

   Latona thence could roam,
With her brave children and defenders near,
In earth, air, sea, or heaven, free of fear;
Here forgave, and Zeus the twins did set,
To guide the sun and moon, as they do yet.

           1830.

TO THE PLANET JUPITER.

Thou art a radiant and imperial star,
Planet! whose silver crest beams bright, afar
Upon the edge of yonder eastern hill,
That, nightlike, seems a third of heaven to fill.
Thou art most worthy of *a poet's* song,
One like a king above the common throng;
And yet thou smilest as if *I* might sing,
Weak as I am, my lyre unused to ring
Among the thousand harps that thrill the world.

The sun's last breath upon the sky has curled,
Flushing the clouds; and now thou hast arisen,
And in the East thy burning eye doth glisten:
Thou whom the ancients held to be a king
Among the Gods. As though thou wast a spring
Of inspiration, I would soar and drink
While yet thou lingerest on the mountain's brink.—
Who bade men say that thou, oh silver Peer!
Wast to the moon a servitor, anear
To sit and watch her eye for messages
Like to the other silver-winged bees,
That swarm around her, when she sits her throne?
Out on the moon! She bringeth storm alone,

At new and full, and every other time;
She turns men's brains, making them madly rhyme,
And rave, and sigh away their weary life;
And shall she be of young adorers rife,
And thou have none?—Nay, *one* will sing to thee
In rudest strains, bending the humble knee.—
Lo! on the edge of the great Western Plain,
The Star of Love doth lingering remain,
She of the ocean-foam, watching thy look,
As one that gazes on an antique book,
Earnestly reading, in the deep, dead night,
Filching from Time his hours.   Ah! sweet delay!
And now she sinks, pursuing the swift day,
Content with thy one glance of answering love:—
Where Venus worships, can I heedless prove?

Now as thou swimmest higher into sight,
Marking the water with a line of light,
     On wave and ripple quietly aslant,
Thy influences steal upon the heart,
With a sweet magic and resistless art,
     Like the still growth of a young vigorous plant.
The mother, watching by her sleeping child,
Blesses thee, when thy light, serene and mild,
Falls through the lattice on her babe's pale face,
Tinging it with a sweet benignant grace,
Like the white shadow of an angel's wing.

The sick man that has lain for many a day,
And wasted like a lightless flower away,
Blesses thee, too, oh JOVE! when thou dost shine
Upon his face with influence divine,
Soothing his thin, blue eyelids to calm sleep.
The child its peevish murmuring will keep
In its vexed nurse's arms, till thou dost glad
Its eyes, and then it sleeps. The thin and sad
And patient student, closes his worn books
A space or so, to gain from thy kind looks
Refreshment: Prisoners in dungeons pent
Climb to the grates, and there with head upbent
Gaze long at thee; the timid deer awake,
And by thy light ramble through fell and brake,
Whistling their joy to thee, the speckled trout
From under his dark rock comes shooting out,
Turns his quick eye to thee, loves thy soft light,
And sleeps within it; the gray water-plant
Looks up to thee beseechingly, aslant,
And thou dost feed it there beneath the wave.
Even the tortoise crawls from his damp cave,
And feeds wherever, on the dewy grass,
Thy light has lingered: nay, thy mild rays pass
To water-depths, and the small coral-fly
Works cheerfully when flattered by thine eye.
Thou touchest not the rudest heart in vain;
Even the sturdy sailor and hard swain

Are grateful when, after a storm, thine eye
Opens amid torn clouds, and calms the sky.
The lover praises thee, to thy sweet light
Likens his love, so tender and more bright,
And tells his mistress thou dost kindly mock
Her radiant eyes. Thou dost the heart unlock,
With care and woe long dark and comfortless,
So that the wretched thy sweet soothing bless,
And cease to long for quiet in the grave.
The lunatic, that to the moon doth rave,
Sleeps in thy light, and is again himself;
The miser pauses as he counts his pelf,
When through the steel-barred windows flash thy glances,
And even him thy loveliness entrances.
Ah! while thy silver arrows pierce the air,
And, far below thee, all the dark woods, where
The wind sleeps, and the mountains crowned with snow,
And the great Sea, whose pulses come and go,
Are still as death,—ah! bring me back again
The bold and happy heart that blessed me, when
Life was delight; before one hope was veiled
By disappointment. Then my cheek was paled,
But not with care;—for late at night and long
I toiled and moiled to gain myself among
Old tomes some knowledge; as indeed I did.
I studied much, and things the wise had hid
In their quaint books I learned; and then I thought

Myself a poet, and I fondly wrought
My boyish feelings into verse, and rained
The loose leaves on the wind, and so I gained
Some praise, and a slight name.

And then I dreamed,—
Ah, me! how like reality it seemed!—
Of loving and being loved, of eyes that shone,
Bright as the Southern Cross, for me alone;—
But I awoke, the vision fled away,
And round me closed a long, cold winter day,
With frost and sleet, since when my poor feet bled
On the sharp flints:—Ah, Jove! couldst thou but lead
Me back to boyhood for a time, it were
Indeed a gift.

THOU, who didst thus *their* destiny control,
I worship thee, hoping that in my soul
Thy light may sink.   Oh, JOVE, I am full sure,
None feel for thy fair star a love more pure,
Than I.   Thou hast been, everywhere, to me
A source of inspiration.   I should be
Sleepless, could I not first behold thine orb,
In East or West.   Then doth my heart absorb,
Like other withering flowers, thy light and life.
For that neglect which cutteth like a knife,
Thou chill'st not with; unless the azure lake

Of heaven is clouded. Planet! thou wouldst make
Of me, as of thine ancient worshippers,
A poet; but, alas! whatever stirs
My tongue and pen, both are but faint and weak.
Apollo hath not, in some gracious freak,
Inspired me with the spirit of his lyre,
Or touched my soul with his ethereal fire.
So that whatever humble song I sing,
To thee is but a meagre offering.
All I can give is small. Thou wilt not scorn
My all. I give no golden sheaves of corn;
I burn to thee no rich and odorous gums;
I offer up to thee no hecatombs;
I build no altars: 'tis a heart alone;
Such as it is, receive it! 'tis thine own.

1833.

LINES WRITTEN ON THE ROCKY MOUNTAINS.

The deep transparent sky is full
     Of many thousand glittering lights,
Unnumbered stars that calmly rule
     The dark dominions of the night;
The mild, sad moon has upward risen,
     Out of the gray and boundless plain;
And all around the white snows glisten,
     Where frost and ice and silence reign,
While ages roll away, and they unchanged remain.

These mountains, piercing the blue sky,
     With their eternal cones of ice;
These torrents, dashing from on high,
     O'er rock and crag and precipice,
Change not, but still remain as ever,
     Unwasting, deathless and sublime,
And will remain, while lightnings quiver,
     Or stars these hoary summits climb,
Or rolls the thunder-chariot of eternal Time.

It is not so with all. I change
     And waste as with a living death,
Like one that has become a strange
     Unwelcome guest, and lingereth

Among the memories of the past,
　　Where he is a forgotten name.
For time hath mighty power to blast
　　The hopes, the feelings, and the fame,
To make the passions swell, or their wild fierceness tame.

The swift wind whistles shrill and loud,
　　And cools my fever-heated brow;
Such was I once, as free, as proud,
　　And yet, alas! how altered now!
And while I gaze upon the plain,
　　These mountains, this eternal sky,
The scenes of boyhood come again,
　　And pass before the vacant eye,
Still wearing something of the shape I knew them by.

Yet why lament?　For what are wrong,
　　False friends, cold hearts, sharp words, deceit,
And life already spun too long,
　　To one who walks with bleeding feet
The world's rough paths?　All will but make
　　Death sweeter, when he comes at last.
Although the outraged heart may ache,
　　Its agony of pain is past,
And patience makes it firm, while life is ebbing fast.

Perhaps, when I have passed away,
   Like the sad echo of a dream,
There may be some one found to say
   A word that will like sorrow seem.
THAT I would have—one genuine tear,
   One kindly and regretful thought,
Grant me but that; and even here,
   In this lone, strange, unpeopled spot,
To breathe away this life of pain I murmur not.

1832.

ODE.

When shall the nations all be free,
  And Force no longer reign;
None bend to brutal Power the knee,
  None hug the gilded chain?
No longer rule the ancient Wrong,
The Weak be trampled by the Strong?—
How long, dear God in heaven! how long,
  The people wail in vain?

Do not th' Archangels on their thrones,
  Turn piteous looks to thee,
When round them thickly swarm the groans
  Of those that would be free?
Of those that know they have the right
To Freedom, though crushed down by Might,
As all the world hath to the light
  And air which Thou mad'st free?

The ancient Empires staggering drift
  Along Time's mighty tide,
Whose waters, running broad and swift,
  Eternity divide:

How many years shall pass, before
Over their bones the sea shall roar,
The salt sand drift, the fresh rains pour,
    The stars mock fallen Pride?

What then the great Republic's fate?
    To founder far from land,
And sink with all her glorious freight,
    Smitten by God's right hand?
Or shall she still her helm obey
In calm or storm, by night or day,
No sail rent, no spar cut away,
    Exultant, proud and grand?

The issues are with God. To do,
    Of right belongs to us:
May we be ever just and true,
    For nations flourish thus!—
JUSTICE is mightier than ships;
RIGHT, than the cannon's brazen lips;
And TRUTH, averting dark eclipse,
    Makes fortunes prosperous.

July 4, 1853.

SPRING.

O, thou delicious Spring!
Nursed in the lap of thin and subtle showers,
  Raining from clouds exhaled from dews that cling
To odorous beds of rare and fragrant flowers,
    And honeysuckle bowers,
  That over grassy walks their tendrils fling:
      Come, gentle Spring!

Thou lover of soft winds!
That wander from the invisible upper sea
  Whose foam the clouds are, when young May unbinds
Her dewy hair, and with sweet sympathy
    Makes crisp leaves dance with glee,
  Even in the teeth of that old sober hind,
      Winter unkind.

Come to us! for thou art
Like the pure love of children, gentle Spring,
  Filling with delicate pleasure the lone heart;
Or like a modest virgin's welcoming;
    And thou dost bring
  Fair skies, soft breezes, bees upon the wing,
      Low murmuring.

Red Autumn, from the South,
Contends with thee. What beauty can he show?
What are his purple-stained and rosy mouth,
And nut-brown cheeks, to thy soft feet of snow,
And exquisite fresh glow,
Thy timid flowers, in their sweet virgin growth
And modest youth?

Hale Summer follows thee,
But not with beauty delicate as thine;—
All things that live rejoice thy face to see;
But when he comes, they pant for heat, and pine
.   For arctic ice, and wine
Thick-frozen, sipped under a shady tree,—
With dreams of thee.

Come, sit upon our hills,
Wake the chilled brooks, and send them down their side,
To make the valleys smile with sparkling rills;
And when the stars into their places glide,
And Dian sits in pride,
I, too, will breathe thine influence that thrills
The grassy hills.

Alas! sweet Spring!—not long
Wilt thou remain, lament thee as we may;
   For as rude Summer waxes stout and strong,
Thou wilt grow thin and pale, and fade away
     As dreams flit, scared at day;
   Thou wilt no more to us or earth belong,
      Except in song.

     So I, who sing, shall die,
Worn thin and pale, perhaps, by care and sorrow;
   And, fainting, with a soft, unconscious sigh,
Bid unto this poor body that I borrow,
     A long good-by,—tomorrow
   To enjoy, I hope, eternal Spring on high,
      Beyond the sky.

1829.

NOON IN SANTA FÉ.

The sun shines dull in the mist amid,
  That, like a grief, is shading him;
And though the mountains be not hid,
  Their distant blue is faint and dim,
Yet marking with their outline deep
  The paler blue that bends above.
The winds have moaned themselves to sleep,
  And scarcely now their soft wings move,
With an unquiet, slumberous motion,
  Watched by the pale, mute, flitting Noon,—
That wanderer of Earth and Ocean,
  Whose stay all men desire, but none obtain the boon.

It is the hour for saddened thought,
  When all things have a softened tone,—
A dream-like indistinctness, fraught
  With all that makes man feel alone.
Perhaps the hour and time it is,
  That in the sad and dreaming heart
Make gray Time's ancient images
  Into a new distinctness start;
Till all that I have lost or left, ,
  Or loved or worshipped in my youth,
Comes up like an unwelcome gift,
  With all the sad and stern reality of truth.

The troubled image of the Past,
    Its buried years, before me rise;
And gazing in the distant vast,
    Dim shapes I see, with saddened eyes,
Like those that I have known before,
    But altered, as I, too, have changed:
Many that near my heart I wore,
    Some long ago from me estranged.
Ah! yes! I know that sad fair face,
    That matchless form, that witchery,
Thy step of air, thy winning grace,—
    I see thee, loved one! in the dim obscurity.

Fair Fancy, Memory's sister, weaves
    No golden web of hope for me,
Or, if she smile, she still deceives
    With all a wanton's mockery;—
She points me to a fireless hearth,
    And,—that most sharp and bitter sting,
We feel upon the lonely earth,—
    Cold looks and colder welcoming:
Friends washed off by life's ebbing tide,
    Like sands along the shifting coasts,
The soul's first love another's bride;
    And other melancholy thoughts that haunt like ghosts.

Well, I have chosen my own rough way,
    And I will walk it manfully;
And do the best that mortal may,
    Wherever duty leadeth me.
No heart that is not wholly cold,
    Can help but love, can help but hate;
What malice knows will sure be told,—
    Libels on all distinction wait:
But as the misty mountain-mane
    Doth not for ever shade its blue,
So vanishes each slander-stain
    From all who earnestly and well their duty do.

1832.

*ARIEL.

I.

I had a dream: Methought Ariel came,
   And bade me follow him; and I arose:
Lighter my body seemed than subtle flame,
   Or than the invisible wind that always blows
Above the clouds. So upward I did aim,
   With quick flight, as the sky-lark sunward goes,—
Led by the Splendor of Ariel's wing,
Whose snowy light before fled, glittering.

II.

So, floating upward through the roseate air,
   And through the wide interstices of cloud,
We climbed the mist-hills, till we halted, where
   The frowning peaks beneath the azure glowed;
Then gazed I all around;—no sun blazed there,
   But crimson light through the pure ether flowed,
And dimmed the moon's eye and the stars' white cones,
Till they were scarce seen on their golden thrones.

---

*This beautiful poem is said to have been written in the prairie
while the author's horse was feeding by his side.

74

III.

Awhile we trod along the quivering peaks
    Of foaming cloud; over entangled rifts
Of purple light; through crimson-misted breaks;
    And saw blue lightning crouching in white drifts,
Restless and quivering, while the broad, deep lakes
    Of vapor tremble as he stirs and shifts,
Waked by the diapason of the thunder,
That swells upon the wild wind rushing under.

IV.

And moored within a labyrinthine bay
    Girded by massive foam-cliffs, rough, storm-worn,
On a flat shore of leaden vapor, lay
    A boat carved out of orange mist, which morn
Had hardened into crystal, many a day,
    Deep in a rift in a vast glacier torn:—
We stepped on board,—we loosed her from the bank,
Our thirsty sail, spread wide, the breezes drank.

V.

And swiftly then our winged bark flew on,
    While I sat looking downward from the prow;
Down broad, shade-margined rivers, dark and dun,
    Over smooth lakes, sea-green, with golden glow,

75

Flecked with broad black spots, here and there, upon
    Their mirrored surface:—now we float below
Like a fleet shadow, over the vext breast
Of boundless, billowy oceans of white mist.

VI.

Then rushed we into chasms, deep, wide and black,—
    By huge, bleak, stormy mountains, of the foam
And rolling masses of the thunder-rack;
    Dark, quivering precipices of deep gloom,
Aeries of brooding lightning;—and did tack
    In narrow inlets, through which roared the boom
Of the mad wind; wherein did Thunder dream,
And on the far blue waves his lightnings gleam.

VII.

And then we issued to the open vast
    Of cloudless air above; and while the sail
Its silver shade upon my forehead cast,—
    Like lightning or swift thought, before the gale
Fled our bright barque. Strange wonders there we passed,
    Currents of astral light, cold, thin and pale,
Strange, voiceless birds that never sink to earth,
And troops of fairies, dancing in mad mirth.

VIII.

Then we descended, till our barque did float
   Above the peak of one lone mountain; and
Ariel furled the sail, and moored our boat
   Upon the margin of a narrow strand
Of undulating mist, that from remote
   And dangerous seas had come, o'er many a land,—
An amaranthine effluence of ocean,
Changing forever with eternal motion.

IX.

Then, bending from the helm, Ariel gazed
   With keen eyes downward through the mighty vast
And waved his hand. The piles of mist upraised,
   That on the mountain's lofty crown were massed;
And, gazing earthward, eager and amazed,
   While either way the rent clouds slowly passed,
I saw a mighty palace, reared upon
The grey, scarred summit of that towering cone.

X.

Columns of gold, with emerald inwrought,
   Ruby and jasper, and infoliate
With leaves of silver, intricate as thought;
   Statues of gold, intercolumniate;

77

Great altars, fed with costly odours, bought
    With toil and blood; and round the rude doors wait
Large hosts of slaves, bending the patient knee,
As though they lingered there some King to see.

XI.

"Here," said Ariel, "liveth Tyranny,
    Remorseless reveller in war and blood;
And these that humbly bend the supple knee,—
    Within whose inmost heart-cells ever brood
Hatred, despair, chill fear and misery,
    Peopling with terrors the sad solitude,—
These are his slaves. They bow there, night and day,
And costly homage to his altars pay."

XII.

"And now, behold! forth from his broad gates ride
    His kindred fiends, the tools of his fierce ire,
Your glorious Republic to divide,
    Friend against friend, the son against the sire,
And near their graves who for your freedom died,
    Slay with the sword and devastate with fire:
And I have brought thee here, that thou mayest tell
Thy countrymen to shun that purple Hell."

XIII.

Then, with a roar like thunder, open flew
  The brazen gates, and all the mountain quivered,
And trembled like a child; and far off, through
  The distant hills, against the grey rocks shivered,
That awful sound; and a wild voice that grew
  A terror to me, surging up, delivered,
In tones that like a brazen trumpet roared,
The order for the march:—Forth came the horde!

XIV.

First came Ambition, with his discous eye,
  And tiger-spring, and hot and eager speed,
Flushed cheek, imperious glance, demeanour high;—
  He in the portal striding his black steed,
Stained fetlock-deep with red blood not yet dry,
  And flecked with foam, did the wild cohort lead
Down the rough mountain, heedless of the crowd
Of slaves that round the altar-steps yet bowed.

XV.

Next came red Rashness, with his restless step,
  In whose large eyes glowed the fierce fire that boiled
In his broad chest. Large gouts of blood did drip
  From his drawn sword; the trembling slaves recoiled:

79

Scorn and fierce passion curled his writhing lip;
 His dress was torn with furious haste, and soiled;—
So, springing on his reeking steed, he shook
The reins, and downward his swift journey took.

XVI.

Then came dark Disappointment, with the foam
 Of rage upon his lips, sad step and slow,
Stern, wrinkled brow, clenched teeth, and heavy gloom,
 Like a shadow on his eyes, in these a glow
Like that of baleful stars within a tomb;
 His tangled locks left in the wind to blow;
And so did he forth from the palace stride,
And stalk away down the steep mountain-side.

XVII.

Next followed Envy, with deep-sunken eye,
 Glaring upon his mates. He beat his breast
And gnashed his teeth, with many a bitter sigh;
 For in his heart, deep in its core, a nest
Of fiery scorpions gnawed, that never die,
 Writhing and stinging ever;—on he pressed,
Mounted upon a pale and hound-eyed steed,
And down the mountain, snarling, did proceed.

XVIII.

And then old Avarice, tottering out, appeared,
   With wrinkled front and gray and matted hair,
And elfish eyes, blue-circled, small and bleared:
   He slowly walked, with cautious, prying air.
Working his lips under his filthy beard,
   Peering upon the ground with searching eye,
Clutching a purse with yellow, wasted hand,—
And so he followed the descending band.

XIX.

Then came Corruption, with his serpent-tongue,
   Quick, hurried gate, and eye astute, yet bold;
And while, amid the crouching, base, bowed throng
   Of suppliant slaves, he did his quick way hold,
He loudly hurried Avarice along,
   Who crawled before him with his bag of gold;
Bestriding then his rich-apparelled steed,
He followed swiftly where his mates did lead.

XX.

Next, dark Fanaticism, his haggard face
   Flushing with holy anger, down the track
Went, loud bewailing that the good old days
   Of fire and faggot had not yet come back,

When Error was a crime, and to the ways
   Of Truth men were persuaded by the rack;—
On either side, a little in advance,
Bigotry rode, and harsh Intolerance.

XXI.

Hypocrisy came next, prim, starched and staid,
   With folded hands and upturned pious eyes,
As though God's law he punctually obeyed;
   His sordid greed seeks its base end by lies;
He lusts for every ripe, voluptuous maid,
   Then wrings his hands, and prays, and loudly cries,
"Owner of men! stand off, afar, while I,
"Holier than thou art, piously pass by!"

XXII.

And next came Treason, with his blood-stained hand,
   Deep, black, fierce eye, and bold, unquailing air;
While even as he passed his hot breath fanned
   The grovelling slaves into rebellion there:
His armour clashed, and his broad battle-brand
   Did in the purple sheen like lightning glare;
And so his fiery courser he bestrode,
The echo of whose hoofs roared down the road.

XXIII.

Last came King Anarchy. His cold eyes flashed
   With red fire blazing up from Hell's abyss;
His large white wolf-teeth angrily he gnashed,
   His blue lips parted like a tigress's:
His dusky destrier was with foam besplashed,
   And fiery serpents did around him hiss,
Writhing amid his war-steed's misty mane,
Whose hoofs the young grass scorched like fiery rain.

XXIV.

As he rode down, there mustered in the rear
   A hideous flock, some few in human form,
Some shapeless. Here came, crouching by, pale Fear,
   Revenge and Wrath, and Rapine, a base swarm;
And Cruelty and Murder, and their peer,
   Red Persecution, pouring a hot storm
Of fire and blood from his relentless hand;—
All these are under Anarchy's command.

XXV.

When the horde passed below the mountain's brow,
   With clashing hoof, mad turmoil and loud din,
Within the hall there rose a wild halloo,
   As though a thousand fiends rejoiced therein;—

The upper air vibrated it unto,
 The currents trembled of its crimson sheen;
The lightning-lofts were shaken; and our boat
Rocked on the strand where the harsh echo smote.

XXVI.

Then did Ariel lift the snowy sail,
 Of our ethereal barque. The helm he took,
And up behind us sprang a gentle gale,
 Murmuring astern, like a sweet summer-brook,
That broad-leaved water-plants from daylight veil;—
 And, while the sail a snowy brightness shook
Upon the prow, I lay and watched the boat,
Steered by Ariel, on its voyage float.

XXVII.

Then, passing swiftly with a favoring gale,
 Round the grey forehead of the storm-scarred hill,
We did descend. Near us the moonlight pale
 Slept in thick masses, soberly and still,
In the deep nooks of many a purple vale,
 Of frosted mist; and down a ringing rill
Of sunlight, flowing past a lofty bank
Of amber cloud, toward the green earth we sank.

XXVIII.

And then we passed by mountain-nourished rivers,
   Vexed to white foam by rocks their sides that galled;
Near hoary crags, by lightning split to shivers,
   Peopled by nervous eagles, grey and bald;
Forests wherein the wind-wave always quivers,
   Shaking their deep hearts green as emerald;
Lakes that, like woman's bosom, panting swell,
Robed with the living foam of asphodel.

XXIX.

Within the shadow of old crumbling columns,
   Along these lakes we sailed, and saw beneath
Great water-snakes rolling their scaly volumes
   Among the water-vines that there did wreathe;—
Through chasms of purple gloom, with rivers solemn
   Moaning between their jagged, rocky teeth;—
And then again above the earth we lifted,
And lowered the sail, and helmlessly there drifted.

XXX.

Below us, stretching from the broad green sea
   Into wide prairies, did a fair land lie,
Studded with lakes as still as porphyry
   And blue hills sleeping in the bluer sky,

From whose white cones' serene sublimity
   The snowy lightning dazzled the sun's eye;
The amethystine rivers thence rolled down
To fling their foam on Ocean's hoary crown.

XXXI.

Great cities, queen-like, stood upon his shore,
   And on the banks of those majestic rivers,
And near broad lakes, where at the awful roar
   Of one great cataract the stunned earth shivers:
Ships went and came in squadrons, flocking o'er
   That Ocean which the Old and New World severs,
Shading the bays and rivers with their sails,
Their starred flags laughing at propitious gales.

XXXII.

Broad fields spread inland, robed in green and gold,
   And waving with a mighty wealth of grain,
From where the bear snarled at the Arctic cold,
   To the Mexique Gulf, and the Pacific Main;—
Far South, in snowy undulations, rolled,
   With their white harvests many a treeless plain;
And where the Sierra westwardly inclines,
Gleamed a new Ophir, with its glittering mines.

XXXIII.

The Throne of Liberty stood in that land,
   Its guards the Law and Constitution; these,
These and no other held supreme command,
   And everywhere, through all the land, was peace.
Grim Despotism fast in his iron hand
   Held all men's rights in the ancient Monarchies;
But Freedom reigned here undisturbed and calm,
Holding an eagle on her snowy palm.

XXXIV.

Then, as I gazed, it seemed men's hearts became
   Transparent to me as the crimsoned air,
Or as the thin sheet of a subtle flame;
   And I could see the passions working there
Like restless serpents; how they went and came,
   And writhed or slept within their fiery lair;
So that I saw the cause of each vibration
That shook the heart-strings of that youthful nation.

XXXV.

I watched the souls of all that people, when
   That train of fiends did thitherward repair;
I saw old creeping Avarice crouch therein,
   Like a caged panther; and his grizzled hair

Choked up the springs of Virtue, so that men
  Were proud the Devil's livery to wear,
And did begin to count and calculate
That Union's value which had made them great.

XXXVI.

I saw red Rashness and Ambition urge
  Men to ill deeds for office; with a wing
Like the free eagle's, lo! they swift emerge
  From the dens and caves of earth, and upward spring,
With daring flight; but like the baffled surge,
  That doth against a rock its masses fling,
They are repelled; some great, calm, kingly eye
Withers their plumes; a little while they fly,

XXXVII.

And then, still striving with their shrivelled wings,
  Drop on the earth, and in each cankered soul
Pale Disappointment crouches, Envy clings,
  Rage, Hate, Despair at the sweet sunlight scowl,
Revenge and fiery Anger dart their stings
  Into themselves, and with the sharp pain howl;
Then forth these patriots go, a motley brood,
And preach sedition to the multitude.

XXXVIII.

Then Faction and the Lust for office shook
   Their filthy wings over the whole land, lighting
On hill and plain, by river, lake and brook
   The fires of discord, and new hates exciting;
And lean Corruption sneaked in every nook,
   With Avarice's hoards to crime inviting;
Till men no longer saw that glittering Star,
The Constitution, shining from afar.

XXXIX.

Fanaticism preached a new crusade,
   And Bigotry damned slavery as a crime;
Intolerance, brandishing his murderous blade,
   Denounced the Southron in bad prose and rhyme;
The Pulpit preached rebellion; men, dismayed,
   Saw the red portents of a bloody time
Burn ominous upon the Northern sky,
And sword-like comets, threatening, blaze on high.

XL.

Treason, without disguise, all clad in mail,
   Stalked boldly over the distracted land:
Cries of Disunion swelled on every gale;
   The Ship of State drew near the rocky strand,

With rent sails, through the lightning and the hail;
  Her mariners a reckless, drunken band;
And Freedom, shuddering, closed her eyes, and left
Their vessel on the weltering seas to drift.

XLI.

Then Anarchy turned loose his maddened steed,
  Whose iron hoofs went clanging through the land,
Filling men's hearts with fear and shapeless dread;
  Then leaped on board, and with audacious hand,
Grasped he the helm, and turned the vessel's head
  Toward unknown seas, and, at his fierce command,
Through the red foam and howling waves, the dark,
Ill-visaged mariners to ruin sailed the barque.

XLII.

I shuddered for a time, and looked again,
  Watching the day of that eventful dawn;
Wild War had broken his adamantine chain,
  Bestrid the steed of Anarchy, and drawn
His bloody scimiter; a fiery rain
  Of blood poured on the land, and scorched the corn;
Wild shouts, mad cries, and frequent trumpets rang,
And iron hoofs thundered with constant clang.

XLIII.

I saw and heard no more, for I did faint,
 And would have fallen to the earth, had not
Ariel stooped and caught me as I went.
 He raised the sail, and left that fearful spot;
And while into the soft, cool air I leant,
 Drinking the wind that followed the swift boat,
He said to me with gentle voice and clear,
Ringing like tones æolian in my ear:

XLIV.

"Thou hast not seen the woes that are to come,
 The long, dark days, that lengthen into years,
The reign of rapine, when the laws are dumb,
 The bloody fields, the hearth-stones wet with tears;
The starving children, wrangling for a crumb,
 The cries of ravished maidens, that God hears,
And does not heed, the blackened walls that stand
Amid the graves, through all the wasted land.

XLV.

"Go, tell your misled people the sad fate,
 The bitter woes and sharp calamities,
That in the swiftly-coming Future wait;
 The fruit of Faction's sordid villainies,

91

Of discord and dissension, greed and hate,
  And all that in man base and brutal is;
Unless they guard, with sleepless vigilance,
Their liberties against such dire mischance."

XLVI.

He said no more; meanwhile we kept along
  The elemental greenness of the ocean,
Whose great breast throbbed and trembled with the strong
  Stern pulses of its vibratory motion;
Across still bays, mid many a tangled throng
  Of misty isles, sleeping like sweet devotion
In woman's heart, bordered with low white shores,
Running off inland with green level floors.

XLVII.

We saw grey water-plants that fanned the deep,
  With golden hair, far down beneath the boat;
Caverns, shell-paven, where the Naiads sleep;
  Clouds of thick light through the great Vast that float;
Great emerald-rifts, wherein the ripples keep
  A constant murmur of æolic notes;
Broad beds of coral, rosy as the Dawn,
The radiant sea-flowers thick on many a lawn.

XLVIII.

And then we left the boat, and quick descended,
　　Through the clear air, as we had first arisen,
Unto my home, wherein I found extended
　　That which again became my sad soul's prison;
Then with a brief adieu he upward wended,
　　While far behind long lines of light did glisten;
Leaving me meditating on my dream,
Which still like deep and dark realty doth seem.

1833.

INVOCATION.

What cheer, Imperial Mountain? Titan, hail!
  Thy distant crest gleams in the morning light,
Like a small shallop's broad and snowy sail,
  Over still waters urging its swift flight.
What cheer, old thunder-scarred and wrinkled peak!
On which the elements in vain their fury wreak?

On thy wide shoulders rests the eternal snow,
  Wherein broad rivers have their hidden springs;
Down thy rough sides impetuous torrents flow,
  The cataract with sullen thunder rings,
And flashing fiercely round thine aged feet,
Against thy patient rocks the fretted waters beat.

Through the dark foam and fluctuating surge,
  That ever dash thy rugged breast upon,
Thou dost in silent majesty emerge,
  Lifting thy forehead proudly to the sun:
Like a great truth, simple, and yet sublime,
Gleaming above the surge of Error and of Time.

Thou standest there for ever, day and night,
  Like a great man, calm, self-possessed, serene;
Who, doing what he knoweth to be right,
  Stands up, firm-footed, earnest, and sincere,
Calmly the suffrage of the world contemns,
Seeks not its worthless praise, nor heeds if it condemns.

Above the Northern Cordilleras towers
  Thy haughty crest, like some strong feudal King,
Elect of Principalities and Powers,
  To whom far isles unwilling tributes bring;
Who holds with pomp and majesty his court,
Among the mail-clad Barons that his throne support.

Thou standest firm there, like an iron will,
  Triumphant over time and circumstance,
Sternly resolved its duty to fulfill,
  And ever towards its object to advance;
While careless of the clamorous hounds that bay,
Through all impediments it marches on its way.

How many ages is it, since the snows
    First on thy forehead and wide shoulders fell?
How many since the wandering sun arose,
    Wondering at thee, grim-visaged sentinel!
On the wide desert's western margin set,
To watch its solemn loneliness, as thou dost yet?

Wast thou an island in the overflow
    Of the great flood?   Did any from afar
Look wistfully to thy eternal snow,
    Over new oceans gleaming like a star?
Or did the waves thee also overwhelm,
Last spot of earth in the wide waters' angry realm.

Howe'er it be, still thou art planted there,
    As when the Deluge round thee ceased to roar;
Thy snows the bright hues of the morning wear:
    The crimson glories of spring-sunrise pour
On thy white brow that proudly fronts the sky,
Bidding a calm defiance to Day's burning eye.

Fierce storms for centuries against thee dash,
  On thy bare head rain torrents of sharp hail,
The baffled lightnings round thy temples flash,
  Over thee roar the thunder and the gale.
What matter to the calm and well-poised soul,
Though round it slander howl, and persecution roll.

The tempests vanish. The round moon shines bright;
  In Heaven's glad ear the cataract's grave hymn
Sounds, through the solemn silence of the night:
  Around thy brow the white stars thickly swim,
Anxious thine aged solitude to cheer,
Even as a wife's fond eyes shine, earnest and sincere.

So all the storms and clouds that gather round
  A great man's reputation, pass away,
And leave it with a brighter glory crowned;
  Above the elemental surge and spray,
To shine on distant ages, far across
The stormy sea of Time, on whose wild waves they toss.

1844.

ODE TO THE MOCKING-BIRD.

Thou glorious mocker of the world! I hear
  Thy many voices ringing through the glooms
Of these green solitudes; and all the clear,
Bright joyance of their song enthralls the ear,
  And floods the heart. Over the sphered tombs
Of vanished nations roll thy music-tide:
  No light from History's starlit page illumes
The memory of these nations: They have died:
    None care for them but thou; and thou mayst sing,
    Over me, too, perhaps, as thy notes ring
Over their bones by whom thou once wast deified.

Glad scorner of all cities! Thou dost leave
  The world's mad turmoil and incessant din,
Where none in others' honesty believe,
Where the old sigh, the young turn gray and grieve,
  Where misery gnaws the maiden's heart within;
Thou flee'st far into the dark green woods,
  Where, with thy flood of music, thou canst win
Their heart to harmony, and where intrudes
    No discord on thy melodies. Oh, where,
    Among the sweet musicians of the air,
Is one so dear as thou to these old solitudes?

Ha! what a burst was that! The æolian strain
   Goes floating through the tangled passages
Of the still woods; and now it comes again,
A multitudinous melody, like a rain
   Of glassy music under echoing trees,
Close by a ringing lake. It wraps the soul
    With a bright harmony of happiness,
Even as a gem is wrapped, when round it roll
    Thin waves of crimson flame; till we become,
    With the excess of perfect pleasure, dumb,
And pant like a swift runner clinging to the goal.

I can not love the man who doth not love,
   As men love light, the songs of happy birds;
For the first visions that my boy-heart wove,
To fill its sleep with, were that I did rove
   Through the fresh woods, what time the snowy herds
Of morning clouds shrunk from the advancing sun,
   Into the depths of Heaven's blue heart, as words
From the poet's lips float gently, one by one,
    And vanish in the human heart; and then
    I revelled in such songs, and sorrowed, when,
With noon-heat overwrought, the music-gush was done.

I would, sweet bird, that I might live with thee,
  Amid the eloquent grandeur of these shades,
Alone with Nature!—but it may not be:
I have to struggle with the stormy sea
  Of human life until existence fades
Into death's darkness. Thou wilt sing and soar
  Through the thick woods and shadow-chequered glades,
While pain and sorrow cast no dimness o'er
  The brilliance of thy heart; but I must wear,
  As now, my garments of regret and care,
As penitents of old their galling sackcloth wore.

Yet, why complain? What though fond hopes deferred
  Have overshadowed Life's green paths with gloom?
Content's soft music is not all unheard:
There is a voice sweeter than thine, sweet bird,
  To welcome me, within my humble home;
There is an eye, with love's devotion bright,
  The darkness of existence to illume.
Then why complain? When Death shall cast his blight
  Over the spirit, my cold bones shall rest
  Beneath these trees; and from thy swelling breast
Over them pour thy song, like a rich flood of light.

                                        1834.

SIMILES.

I.

Above me snows and ice-crags, and around
   The Cordilleras towering, grand and stern;—
Near me a stream over the black rocks bounding,
Its echoes from the caverned slopes resounding:—
    Off in the distance a blue, grass-rimmed lake,
     Through which the stream shoots, and the slight waves
        make
A soft, low music on the pebbled shore.
   The sun's rays its blue bosom penetrate,
And still the thirsty waters beg for more;
And still the sun, from his exhaustless store,
   Rains down his beams, until, with its full freight,
The lake appears a sheet of silver light
   And liquid diamonds, flashing a full return
Back to the generous sun.
                Thou, fair and bright,
   Star of my soul! for whom for ever burn
The altars of my soul's idolatry,
Let thy soft rays of love into the sea
   Of my sad soul sink and become a part
Of it and of its essence; then shall I,
   Strong with thy strength, and struggling with stout **heart**,
Effect somewhat, before it comes to me to die.

II.

Lo! the great mountain's snowy shoulders gleam,
    Above the clouds, high in the upper air;
Perpetual sentinels the giants seem
    Of the lake's quiet.   Their gray heads are bare
    In God's great presence, which is mighty there,
In the ethereal, thin, keen element.
One floating cloud hath down from heaven leant,
    Far down one slope, and feeds the springing leaves,
And silently condensing into dew,

    Feeds the parched grass that gratefully receives
The welcome gift, and gladly grows anew,
And smiles in the light.

                    Dear lady of my love!
My soul's throned Queen, all empresses above!
    Though distant from me a half a continent,
Where other clouds are floating past the shores
Against which the Atlantic, dashing, roars;

    Be thou like this one, which the Pacific sent,
As tribute to the haughty mountains.   Here,
Like a soft cloud or rosy atmosphere,
Let thy dear love envelope me, and bless
My sad soul's thirsty desert and parched wilderness.

                                            1832.

APOSTROPHE.

Oh, Liberty! thou child of many hopes,
     Nursed in the cradle of the human heart;
While Europe in her glimmering darkness gropes,
     Do not from us, thy chosen ones, depart!
     Still be to us, as thou hast been and art,
The spirit that we breathe! Oh, teach us still
     Thine arrowy truths unquailingly to dart,
Until all tyrants and oppressors reel,
And despotisms tremble at thy thunder-peal!

Methinks thy daylight now is lighting up
     The far horizon of yon hemisphere
With golden lightning. Over the hoary top
     Of the blue mountains see I not appear
     Thy lovely dawn, while Shame, and crouching Fear,
And Slavery perish under tottering thrones?
     How long, oh Liberty! until we hear
Instead of an insulted people's moans,
The crushed and wreathing tyrants uttering deep groans?

Is not thy spirit living still in France?
     Will it not waken soon in storm and fire?
Will earthquakes not 'mid thrones and cities dance,
     And Freedom's altar be the funeral pyre

103

Of tyranny and all his offspring dire?
In Hungary, Germany, Italia, Spain,
And Austria, thy spirit doth inspire
The multitude; and though, too long, in vain,
They struggle in deep gloom, yet slavery's night shall wane.

And shall *we* sleep, while all the earth awakes?
Shall *we* turn slaves, while on the Alpine cones
And vine-clad hills of Europe brightly breaks
The morning-light of Liberty? What thrones
Can equal those which on our fathers' bones
The demagogue would build? What chains so gall,
As those the self-made Helot scarcely owns,
Till they eat deeply; till the live pains crawl
Into his soul, who madly caused himself to fall?

Men's freedom may be wrested from their hands,
And they may mourn; but not like those who throw
Their heritage away; who clasp the bands
On their own limbs, and creeping, blindly go
Like timorous fawns, to their own overthrow.
Shall we thus fall? Is it so difficult,
To *think* that we are free, yet *be* not so?
To shatter down in one brief hour of guilt,
The holy fane of freedom that our fathers built!

1834.

THE ROCKY MOUNTAINS.

"The Mountains, piercing the blue sky,
    With their eternal cones of ice;
These torrents, dashing from on high,
    O'er rock and crag and precipice

Change not, but still remain as ever,
    Unwasting, deathless and sublime,
And will remain, while lightnings quiver,
    Or stars these hoary summits climb,
Or rolls the thunder-chariot of eternal Time."

LINES.

The sun's last light is in the sky,
   His last warm breath is on my brow,
Dark shadows to the mountains high
   Begin to stoop on swift wings now.
The ruddy twilight quivers up
   Above the line of snowy crests,
Like wine that in an agate cup
   From tremulous motion never rests.
The great hills in the south grow blue
   And indistinct, and far away
In the orient their silver hue
   Is changing into sullen gray.
   All objects, where the shadows play,
Grow dim and indistinctly deep,
Tired Nature's eyes now close, and she inclines to sleep.

Into the soul sad fancies swarm,
   As bees swarm, clinging to each other;
Or waves, when memories of storm
   Excite them to devour each other.

105

The dreams of hope, at morning born
    That love the daylight and the sun,
Have fled, and wander far, forlorn,
    Or vanished slowly, one by one:
And all the painful thoughts that rested,
    In deep calm slumber, in the breast
Which many a day they have infested,
    Awake, and bitterly molest
    The heart, their most unwilling nest,
Their home, and worse than all, the food
Of these, the vulture-eyed, and all their ravening brood.

One thought of home is often there,
    Like a lone bird, with sad, deep eyes,
Immovable as dull despair,
    A grief profound that never dies.
Now when Death's influences seem
    On all the universe around,
Now when the sleepy mountains dream,
    Plunged into silence most profound;
When rock and pine, and snow and sky,
    Sleep shaded by Night's dusky wing,
A sleep like death, to man's dim eye
    The self-same awful, sombre thing;
    All these sad influences bring
That melancholy thought again,
And on the heart it falls like a cold winter-rain.

Perhaps death now is busy there,
  And some dear soul that I have loved,
Into the chill and desert air,
  Hath sadly from its home removed.
Perhaps they mourn some loved one dead
  Thinking of me, the absent, too;
While I, unconscious, have not shed
  A tear, nor even their sorrow knew.
Perhaps, whenever I return,
  After my ordered task is done,
Instead of some loved face and form,
  I may but find a simple stone,
  A sister's cold heart set upon;
While they will long before have ceased
To mourn for her whom I shall mourn as just deceased.

'Tis sad to wander all alone
  Through the wide world, a homeless thing,
Like a lost wave that makes its moan,
  And hastens to the land, to fling
Its life away upon the shore,
  With nothing near to mourn its death;
But like the eagle far to soar,
  While Fate his full nest shattereth;
Then to return, and fainting fly
  Round a wrecked home made desolate,
Perhaps to hear his young's last cry,

 The last sob of his dying mate;
    This is the sharpest blow of Fate,
   The most unutterable woe,
Crushing the heart and brain at one tremendous blow.

   This must men bear, as men have borne
     A thousand giant woes beside;
   And should this dearest hope be shorn
     Away, this light, that scarce descried,
   Hath been my beacon-fire of late;
     Still I have much to do in life,
   And manfully must front my fate:
     For duty is a constant strife.
   The branchless tree still liveth on,
     The mastless ship still holds her way,
   Nor heeds the wind, the storm, the sun:
     So will I work all life's brief day,
     Doing my duty as I may:
   And some, perhaps, will mourn my death,
When neither hate prevents, nor envy hindereth.

                         1832.

TO THE MOON.

Oh, quickly rise,
Thou lovely and most welcome Moon!
　Look into my sad eyes,
　Ere sober Night too quickly hies;—
　　And bless me soon!

Here I have kept,
Watching to see thine advent bright,
　While others lay and slept;
　As I at other times have wept,
　　For day's fresh light.

Here I have lain,
And eastward kept my anxious gaze,
　But all thus far in vain:
　No shower of light like silver rain
　　Shines through the haze.

The evening star
Has chidden me, saying, "Get to bed!
　She wanders yet afar,
　Where the great Asian deserts are
　　Inhabited

"By Scythian hordes;
Or where the springs of Indus rise;
Or flash the fiery swords
Of dry Sahara's Arab lords;
Or where the skies

"Smile on the shores
Of Teneriffe, or on old Rome:
Or where the Danube roars
Or, tortured by Venetian oars,
The lagunes foam."

That star has set
Behind the western hills; and thou
Hast not arisen yet,
Though all the silver stars are met
In heaven now.

Ah! here she comes!
And all those silver stars grow pale,
As, swimming through gray glooms,
The queen of love and light illumes
Crag, hill, and dale.

Now I can sleep,
If thou wilt but vouchsafe to shine
    From heaven's abysses deep,
    And pleasantly mine eyelids steep
        In light divine.

    The stars that peer,
Like timid children, from on high,
    (Small pilots they, that steer
    Their sparkling boats around thy sphere),
        Love not as I.

    Adieu! Adieu!
My heavy lids begin to close,
    And from thy domain blue,
    Sleep's gentle and refreshing dew
        Upon them flows.

    Stay in thy flight!
In at my humble casement shine,
    And bless with thy soft light,
    Oh, silver nautilus of night,
        All that is mine!

1830.

NIGHT ON THE ARKANSA*.

Night comes upon the Arkansa with swift stride,—
   Its dark and turbid waters roll along
Bearing wrecked trees and drift,—deep, red, and wide
The heavy forests sleeps on either side,
   To the water's edge low-stooping; and among
   The patient stars the moon her lamp has hung,
Lit with the spirit of the buried sun.
No blue waves dance the stream's dark bosom on,
   Glittering like beauty's sparkling starry tears;
No crest of foam, crowning the river dun,
   Its misty ridge of frozen light uprears:
   One sole relief in the great void appears—
A dark blue ridge, set sharp against the sky,
Beyond the forest's utmost boundary.

Not so wast thou, O, brave old Merrimac!
   As I remember thee; as thou art seen
By the Soul's eyes, when dreaming, I go back
To my old home, and see the small boats tack

---

*The author spelled Arkansas without the final "s," as it appears
here, in his privately printed volume of poems, and it seems to have
been the customary spelling then.

On thy blue waters, gliding swift between
The old gray rocks that o'er them fondly lean,
Their foreheads scarred with lightning. There, around
Grim capes the surly waters whirl and bound;
And here and there grave patriarchal trees
Persuade the grass to clothe the reluctant ground
And frowning banks with green.   Still villages
Sleep in the embraces of the cool sea-breeze:—
Ah, brave old stream!—thou seemest to infold
My heart within thy waters, as of old.

1838.

BUENA VISTA.

From the Rio Grande's waters to the icy lakes of Maine,
Let all exult! for we have met the enemy again:
Beneath their stern old mountains we have met them in
    their pride
And rolled from BUENA VISTA back the battle's bloody tide;
Where the enemy came surging swift, like the Mississippi's
    flood,
And the reaper, Death, with strong arms swung his sickle,
    red with blood.

SANTANA boasted loudly that, before two hours were past,
His Lancers through Saltillo should pursue us fierce and
    fast:—
On comes his solid infantry, line marching after line;
Lo! their great standards in the sun like sheets of silver shine;
With thousands upon thousands,—yea, with more than three
    to one,—
Their forest of bright bayonets fierce-flashing in the sun.

Lo! Guanajuato's regiment, Morelos' boasted corps,
And Guadalajara's chosen troops!—all veterans tried before.
Lo! galloping upon the right four thousand lances gleam,
Where, floating in the morning wind, their blood-red pennons
    stream;
And here his stern artillery climbs up the broad plateau:
Today he means to strike at us an overwhelming blow.

Now, WOOL, hold strongly to the heights! for, lo! the mighty tide
Comes, thundering like an avalanche, deep, terrible, and wide.
Now, ILLINOIS, stand steady! Now, KENTUCKY, to their aid!
For a portion of our line, alas! is broken and dismayed:
Great bands of shameless fugitives are fleeing from the field,
And the day is lost, if Illinois and brave Kentucky yield.

One of O'BRIEN'S guns is gone!—On, on their masses drift,
Till their cavalry and infantry outflank us on the left;
Our light troops, driven from the hills, retreat in wild dismay,
And round us gathers, thick and dark, the Mexican array.
SANTANA thinks the day is gained; for, now approaching near,
MINON'S dark cloud of Lancers sternly menaces our rear.

Now, LINCOLN, gallant gentleman, lies dead upon the field,
Who strove to stay those cravens, when before the storm they
    reeled.
Fire, WASHINGTON, fire fast and true! Fire, SHERMAN, fast
    and far!
Lo! BRAGG comes thundering to the front, to breast the
    adverse war!
SANTANA thinks the day is gained! On, on his masses crowd,
And the roar of battle swells again more terrible and loud.

NOT YET!—Our brave old General comes to regain the day;—
KENTUCKY, to the rescue! MISSISSIPPI, to the fray!

Again our line advances! Gallant Davis fronts the foe,
And back before his rifles, in red waves the Lancers flow.
Upon them yet once more, ye brave!—The avalanche is
  stayed!
Back roll the Aztec multitudes, all broken and dismayed.

Ride! May —To Buena Vista! for the Lancers gain our rear,
And we have few troops there to check their vehement
  career,
Charge, Arkansas! Kentucky, charge! Yell, Porter,
  Vaughan, are slain,
But the shattered troops cling desperately unto that crim-
  soned plain;
Till, with the Lancers intermixed, pursuing and pursued,
Westward, in combat hot and close, drifts off the multitude.

And May comes charging from the hills with his ranks of
  flaming steel,
While shattered with a sudden fire, the foe already reel:
They flee amain!—Now to the left, to stay the torrent there,
Or else the day is surely lost, in horror and despair!
For their hosts pour swiftly onward, like a river in the Spring,
Our flank is turned, and on our left their cannon thundering.

Now, good artillery! bold Dragoons! Steady, brave hearts!
  be calm!—
Through rain, cold hail and thunder, now nerve each gallant
  arm!

What though their shot fall round us here, yet thicker than
the hail?
We'll stand against them, as the rock stands firm against
the gale.
Lo! their battery is silenced! but our iron sleet still showers.
They falter, halt, retreat!—Hurrah! the glorious day is ours!

In front, too, has the fight gone well, where, upon gallant
Lane,
And on stout Mississippi, the thick Lancers charged in vain:
Ah! brave Third Indiana! you have nobly wiped away
The reproach that through another corps befell your State
today;
For back, all broken and dismayed, before your storm of fire,
Santana's boasted chivalry, a shattered wreck, retire.

Now, charge again, Santana! or the day is surely lost—
For back, like broken waves, along our left your hordes are
tossed.
Still faster roar his batteries,—his whole reserve moves on;
More work remains for us to do, ere the good fight is won.
Now for your wives and children, men! Stand ready yet
once more!
Fight for your lives and honors! Fight as you never fought
before!

Ho! HARDIN breasts it bravely! and heroic BISSELL there
Stands firm before the storm of balls that fill the astonished
   air:
The Lancers dash upon them too! The foe swarm ten to one:
HARDIN is slain; McKEE and CLAY the last time see the sun:
And many another gallant heart, in that last desperate fray,
Grew cold, its last thoughts turning to its loved ones, far
   away.

Speed, speed, Artillery! to the front!—for the hurricane of fire
Crushes those noble regiments, reluctant to retire!
Speed swiftly! Gallop! Ah! they come! Again BRAGG
   climbs the ridge,
And his grape sweeps down the swarming foe, as a strong
   man moweth sedge:
Thus baffled in their last attack, compelled perforce to yield,
Still menacing in firm array, their columns leave the field.

The guns still roared at intervals: but silence fell at last,
And on the dead and dying came the evening shadows fast.
And then above the mountains rose the cold moon's silver
   shield,
And patiently and pitying she looked upon the field,
While careless of his wounded, and neglectful of his dead,
Despairingly and sullenly by night SANTANA fled.

And thus on BUENA VISTA'S heights a long day's work was
    done,

And thus our brave old General another battle won.

Still, still our glorious banner waves, unstained by flight or
    shame,

And the Mexicans among their hills still tremble at our name.

So, *honor unto those that stood! Disgrace to those that fled!*

And everlasting glory unto Buena Vista's dead.

February 28, 1847.

AN EVENING CONVERSATION.

One day last spring,—one sunny afternoon,—
Lapt in contented indolence, I lay
Within a pillared circle of old trees;
Deep-bedded in the smooth luxurious sward,
That, fed by dropping dew and faithful shade,
Grew green and thick under the stout, strong oaks.
Around me the broad trees kept watch and ward,
Swinging their foreheads slowly in the air,—
Green islets in an eddying overflow
Of amber light. Among the emerald leaves
The broken waves from that enfolding sea
Struggled to reach the young birds in their nests,
As truth strives earnestly to reach the heart,
Often repulsed, yet still endeavouring.
One strip of light lay on the level grass,
Like a thin drift of pearl-snow, tinged with rose.
There I had lain since noon, stretched out at ease,
Reading by turns, in this and that old book,
Fuller, Montaigne, and good Sir Thomas Browne,
Feltham and Herbert. Mingling with the light,
As in a song mingle two girls' sweet voices,
The song of many a mad bird floated up,
Dazzling my ears, to the high empyrean.
Breaking upon the blue sky's western beach,
Flung upward from the throbbing sea below,

The waves of light and cloud foamed up in spray,
Stained by the sun with all his richest colours,
Sapphire and sardonyx: floating forth, perfumes
From rose and jasmine wandered wide abroad,
Into the meadow, and along the creek,
That dances joyfully along its bed
Of silver sand and pebbles, through the glade.
And like a child, frightened at sudden dusk,
Stops, still as death, under yon dark gray crag,
Of thunder-scarred and overhanging rock,
Where in deep holes lurks the suspicious trout.
The locust-trees, with honey-dropping blooms,
Tempted the bees, that, darting to and fro,
Grew rich apace with their abundant spoil:
And the magnolia, with its sweet perfume,
Within large circle loaded all the air.
My children played around me on the grass,—
Sad rogues, that interrupted much my thought,
And did perplex my reading,—one in chief,
A little chattering girl with bright brown eyes,
Scarce taught to speak distinctly, but my pet,
As she well knew, and of it took advantage.
While there I lay, reading in idle mood,
I heard a step along the shaded walk,
Where the clematis and the climbing rose,
The honeysuckle and the jasmine turned
Their bright eyes to the sun,—an emerald arch,

With golden flowers embroidered. Looking up,
I saw approaching with his kindly smile,
And outstretched hand, the dearest of my friends,
Who played with me in childhood on the sands,
And on the sounding rocks that fringed the sea,
And on the green banks of the Merrimac;
Grew up with me to manhood, with me left
Our ancient home, and many a weary month,
Fast by my side, still toiled and travelled on,
Through desert, forest, danger, over mountains,
Amid wild storms, deep snows,—bore much fatigue,
Hunger and thirst, bravely and like a man.—
After warm welcome kindly interchanged,
Idly we stretched ourselves upon the sward,
And lightly talked of half a hundred things,
Each with a little head upon his arm,
Whose bright eyes looked as gravely into ours,
As though they understood our large discourse:
Until at length it chanced that Luther said,
Responding to some self-congratulation
That bubbled from the fountain of my heart,
At thinking of my humble, happy life:—

    "We are all mariners on the sea of life;
And they who climb above us up the shrouds,
Have only, in their over-topping place,
Gained a more dangerous station, and foothold
More insecure. The wind, that passeth over,
And harmeth not the humble crew below,

Whistleth amid the shrouds, and shaketh down
These overweening climbers of the ocean,
Into the seething waters of the sea.
The humble traveller securely walks
Along green valleys, walled with rocky crags,
Deep-buried vales, in Alps or Apennine,
By Titans sentinelled, yet rich with flowers,
And gushing with cool springs;—a cloudless sun
Lighting his pathway;—while the venturous fool,
Who climbed the neighboring mountain, sees, aghast
The purple drifts of thunder-shaken cloud
Roll foaming over the blue icy crags,
On which his feet slip,—feels the heavy spray
Dash, roaring like a sea, against his side,
And bitterly repents he climbed so high.
Sharp lightning flashes through the billowy dusk
Of the mad tempest. Through the lonely pines,
Far down below him, howls the exulting wind,—
The thunder crashes round his dizzy head,—
And smitten by the earthquake's mailed hand
The jut whereon he stands gives way, like Power,
And down a thousand fathoms headlong falls
The ambitious climber, a bruised, bloody mass,
Before the peaceful traveller below.
Better a quiet life amid our books,
Than, like mad swimmers in a stormy ocean,
To breast the roar and tumult of the world."

"I think so, too: and I am well content
To lead a peaceful, quiet humble life,
Among my children and my patient books.
Disgrace and danger, like two hungry hounds,
Run ever on the track of those who do
Good service to their country, or achieve
Distinction and a name above their fellows.
And slander is an ever-current coin
Easy of utterance as pure gold, deep-stamped
With the king's image, in the mint of Truth.
What service to his country can one do,
In the wild warfare of the present age?
To gain success, the masses must be swayed;—
To sway the masses, one must be well skilled
And dexterous with the weapons of the trade.
Who fights the gladiator without skill,
Fights without arms. Why! he must lie and cheat
By fair pretences, double and turn at will,
Profess whatever doctrine suits the time,
Juggle and trick with words, in everything
Be a base counterfeit, and fawn and crouch
Upon the level of the baser sort.
I love the truth, because it is the Truth,
And care not whether it be profitable,
Or if the common palate relish it.
Of all things most I hate the plausible:
An open knave's an open enemy;

124

But sleek Pretence with the stilletto stabs,
At dusky corners, of a starless night.
The True and Popular are deadly foes,
Ever at dagger's point, in endless feud.
If one could serve his country by success,
Or strengthen her defenses, he might well
Endure abuse and bitter contumely,
Slander and persecution; but to fling
One's self down headlong from the vessel's prow,
Into the angry chasms of the deep,
Without a hope to stay the ship's mad course,
Is the profoundest folly of the time.—
Behold how nobly sets the Imperial Sun!
The golden glories of his mellow rays
On the green meadow-level fall aslant;
On either side, the crests of snowy cloud,
With crimson inter-penetrated, shrink
And yield him room: no dusky bar obscures
The broad magnificence of his wide eye;
Though farther south, dark as a cataract
Of thundering waters, a great cloud lets down
Its curtain to the blue horizon's edge;
While, here and there, a wing of snowy foam,
Upon its front, glints like the shining sail
Of some aerial shallop, fleeing swift
Along the surface of the tranquil deep.—
Will truth at any time shine broadly forth,

Even as the sun shines, with no cloud of Error
To intercept a single glorious ray?"

"Truth is omnipotent, and will prevail;
And Public Justice certain."

"Aye, my friend!
A great man said so. 'Tis a noble thought,
Nobly expressed; itself a creed complete.
But in what sense is Truth omnipotent,
And at what time is Public Justice certain?—
Truth will avenge herself, for every wrong,
And for all treason to her majesty,
Upon the nation or the individual,
That doth the wrong, by those grave consequences,
Which do, from falsehood or in deed or word,
By law inflexible result. The cause
Why nations do so often topple down,
Like avalanches, from their eminence,
Why men do slink into disastrous graves,
In the stern sentence hath been well expressed;
'Ye would not know the truth or follow it.'
Truth has the power to vindicate itself;
But to convince all men that 't is the truth,
Is far beyond its reach: and public virtue
And public service eminent, are paid,
In life, by obloquy and contumely,
But, after death, by large obsequies,
And monuments and mausolea. Thus

Is public justice certain. We regard
With slight observance and a careless glance,
The Sun that now has closed his radiant eye,
Below the dim horizon's dusky verge,
So long as we behold him in the heavens,
And know that God's Omnipotence compels
His due return. We give no earnest thanks
Of heartfelt gratitude for this great gift
Of light, the largest blessing of them all.—
Lo! he has sunk beneath the grassy sea
Of the broad prairie, whose great emerald lid
Shuts slowly over him. If never more
That glorious orb should rise to light the earth,
Men, staggering blindly through unnatural night,
Would understand the blessing they had lost,
And public justice would be done the Sun."

    "After a long, dark night, a starless night,
In which the thin moon early struggled down
To where the sky and desert met together,
Plunging with hard endeavor through the surf
And spray that gloomed along the tortured heaven,—
After a long, dark night of storm and sleet,
The daylight comes with slow and feeble steps.
How imperceptibly the Dawn begins,
After the storm has sobbed itself asleep,
To shine upon the eyelids of the East.
By slow degrees the distant snowy crests

Of the great mountains, where, for age on age,
Tempests have vainly thundered, are discerned
Upheaving their dim heads among the clouds.
The straining eye then makes the contour out
Of the near forests. Then a rosy mist
Spreads like a blush upon the purple clouds
Becoming by degrees a crimson light;
Until, at last, after a weary watch,
Kept by cold voyagers on disastrous seas,
Or storm-vexed travellers on wide desert plains,
The broad sun rushes through the eddying mist,
Flinging it off, as from a frigate's prow
Flash back the sparkling waves. The wakened world,
Gladdened with light, rejoices in her strength,
And men adore the imperatorial Sun.
So shall it be with Truth. Long ages are
The minutes of her twilight. The white sails
Of the Dawn's boat are crimsoned by her light,
Where it lies rocking near the eastern strand,
Waiting a pilot to assume the helm,
And steer it round the circle of the sky;
For Truth below the horizon lingers yet.
But after you and I are dead and cold,
Our bones all mouldered to a little dust,
Our monuments all crumbled into clay,
She, like the sun, shall rise and light the world,
Never to set. The humblest man has power

To accelerate her coming; and the words
We speak or write, in that effect shall live
Long after we are gathered to the dead.
Thought shakes the world, as the strong earthquake's tread
Shakes the old mountains and the impatient sea.
Each written word, teaching the humblest truth,
No matter in what homely garb arrayed,
Is one of those uncounted myriad drops
That makes the stream of Thought, which first spring forth
A slender, feeble rill, when all the earth
Was dark as midnight, from the inmost caves
And deep recesses of the human mind,
Where it was born. Think you one drop is lost
Of all by which that stream has grown so great?—
No longer trickling over the gray rocks,
Or foaming over precipice and crag,
It rolls along, a broad, deep, tranquil stream,
Resistless in calm energy and strength,
Through the wide plains,—and feels the giant pulse,
(So near it is to universal power),
Of Ocean throbbing in its great blue heart.
Let us work on!—for surely it is true
That none work faithfully without result.
What if we do not the result perceive?
God sees it; it is present now, to Him:
So that we know our labour is not lost."

  "Content you friend! I shall not cease to work.
I am the harnessed champion of Truth,

Cuirassed and greaved, sworn to her glorious cause,
With Beauty's favor glittering in my helm
But henceforth I shall labour in the peace
And quietness of my beloved home.
No good is wrought by mingling in the fray
Of party-war. Under these kingly trees,
Encouraged by my children's loving eyes,
Soothed to serene and self-possessed content,
By all the sights and sounds that bless me here,
Will I work ever in her noble cause.
The words of Truth should flow upon the ears
Of the unwilling world, until it heeds:
Even as the crystal waters of our spring,
That, night and day, all seasons of the year,
Indifferent to censure or to praise,
Seen and unseen, singing their quiet tune,
Leap joyfully over its grassy brim,
Starred with bright flowers; rain on the thankful sward,
Where now the almond drops its rosy gems,
And the syringa trails its drooping twigs,
Fringed thickly with its small and snowy blooms;
And murmuring their gratitude to God,
Flow onward, seeking patiently the sea;
Not other now, than when, for many an age,
Primæval forests hid it from all sight,
Save the fond stars; no lip bent down to drink;

And since creation's morning, not an eye
Of man had seen it. 'T is a pregnant lesson."

"I see its waters gleaming in the light
Of the young moon, and hear the slender sound
Of the stirred pebbles in its narrow bed.
If men would do their duty like the springs,
Committing the result and their reward
To God, who loveth all, the golden age,
That most delicious fable of old rhyme,
Would come indeed."

                   "I, for my single self,
Shall still live on in this, the peaceful calm
And golden ease of my dear humble home:
As in the sheltered harbor of some isle,
Enclosed by southern seas, the storm-worn ship
Escaped the waves, old ocean's hungry hounds,
That cry and chafe without, furls all her sails,
And sleeps within the shadow of the trees,
Rocked by the undulations caused by storm,
That vexes all the ocean round the isle.
Here will I make myself a golden age,
Here live content, and happier than a king.
Nor bird that swings and sleeps in his small nest,
Nor bee that revels in the jasmine-blooms,
Nor humming-bird, that robs the honeysuckle,

Nor cricket, nested under the warm hearth,
Shall sing or work more cheerfully than I."
With this, the moon, opening one azure lid,
Had sometime poured her light upon the birds,
Among the green leaves of the ancient oaks;
The drops rained thick upon the bright green grass,
From the spring's brim, like a swift silver hail;
The meadow seemed a wide, clear, level lake
Of molten silver, by her alchemy;
The shoulders of the northern mountains glittered
With a new glory, and one splintered peak
Shot up in bold relief against the sky,
With one large star resting upon his crown,
A beacon-light on a Titanic tower.
Around that peak, to north and east stretched out
The line of dusky forest, far away,
Bounding the prairie like a rampart there,
With curtain, bastion, scarp and counterscarp.
The thick stars smiled upon the laughing earth,
As bright and cheerful as a young child's eyes.
The thin leaves, shaken by the southern wind,
Murmured in night's pleased ear. The light dew fell
On bud and flower; and, wakened by the moon,
The locust and the katydid sang loud
And shrill within the shadows of the trees.
While in the thorn-tree, growing near the spring.
Hid in the drifted snow of its white blooms,

The merry mimic of our southern woods
Poured out large waves of gushing melody,
That overflowed the meadow many a rood,
And undulated through the pillared trees.
Our little audience, fallen fast asleep,
Reminded us of home. So we arose,
And slowly walking to the house, there sat
Near the large windows, where the moon shone in
Upon the carpets, and the Spring's warm breath,
Sweet as a girl's, came heavy with perfume;
And, with a bottle of bright, sparkling wine,
From sunny France, and fitful conversation,
Sustained awhile, then dying into silence,
Prolonged our sitting far into the night.

1845.

DEATH IN THE DESERT.

The sun is sinking from the sky,
  The clouds are clustering round the moon,
Like misty bastions, mountain-high;
  And night approaches, ah! too soon.
Around me the dark prairie spreads
  Its limitless monotony,
And near me, in wide sandy beds,
  Runs water, salter than the sea,
  Bitter as tears of misery.
And now the sharp, keen, frosty dew
  Begins to fall upon my head,
Piercing each shattered fibre through;   .
By it my torturing wound with a fresh pain is fed.

Near me lies dead my noble horse:
  I watched his last convulsive breath,
And saw him stiffen to a corse,
  Knowing like his would be my death.
The cowards left me lying here
  To die; and for three weary days,
I've watched the sunlight disappear:

134

Again I shall not see his rays;
On my dead heart they soon will blaze.
Oh, God! it is a fearful thing
To be alone in this wide plain,
To hear the hungry vulture's wing,
And watch the fainting light of my existence wane.

Am I, indeed, left here to die?
Alone! alone!—It is no dream!
At times I hope it is. Though nigh,
Already faintly sounds the stream.
I *must* die!—and fierce wolves will gnaw
My corpse before the pulse is still,
Before my parting breath I draw.
This doth the cup of torture fill;
This, this it is that sends a thrill
Of anguish through my inmost brain;
This thought, far bitterer than death:
I care not for the passing pain,
But fain would draw in peace my last, my parting breath.

And here, while left all, all alone,
To die, (how strange *that* word *will* sound!)

With many a bitter, mocking tone
    The faces of old friends come round.
They tell of one untimely sent
    Down to the dark and narrow grave,
By Honor's code; of old friends bent
    With grief, for causes that I gave:
    And leaning on each misty wave,
I see the shapes I loved and lost
    Gather around, with deep, dim eyes,
Like drowning men to land uptossed;
And here one mocks, and my vain rage defies.

    Dear God! My children,—spare the thought!
    Bid it depart from me, lest I
At length to madness should be wrought,
    And cursing Thee, insanely die!
Hush! the cold pulse is beating slow,—
    I see death's shadow close at hand;—
I turn from sunset's golden glow,
    And looking toward my native land,
    Where the dark clouds, like giants, stand,
I strain my eyes, and hope, perchance,
    To see beneath the calm, cold moon,
Some shape of human-kind advance,
To give a dying man the last, the saddest boon.

In vain, in vain! No footstep comes!
    All is yet lone and desolate;
Deeper and darker swell the glooms,
    And with them Death and eyeless Fate.
Now am I dying. Well I know
    The pains that gather round the heart.
The wrist's weak pulse is beating slow,
    And life and I begin to part:
    Vain now would be the leech's art:—
But death is not so terrible,
    As it hath been. No more I see!
My tongue is faltering! Now all's well!
soul,—'tis Thine, oh Father!—take it unto Thee!

1883.

TO THE MOCKING-BIRD.

Sweet bird! Thou singest in the lonely woods,
   Far from great cities. There men dream of life,
And walk with blinded eyes, while grim Care broods
   Upon their withered hearts; and snarling Strife,
Flaps her foul wings before the eyes of men,
   Hate gnaws their hearts, and sordid Avarice halts
Out from his noisome, miserable den,
   Clutching men's souls with yellow, shrivelled bands,
Till each shrinks up, and filthy gods exalts
   To proud dominion, worse than Pagan lands
      Ever bowed down before;
While, grasping handfuls of his glittering ore,
   He makes of it, oh, wonder! tough, strong bands,
To bind them to his sordid service and curst lore.

Thou knowest nought of this. Thy home is in
   The thick green forests. There thou hast thy nest,
Where the leaves whisper with an earnest din,
   And gentle winds cool thy harmonious breast,
Andthere thy music fills the listening wood,
   And rings among the giant forest trees,

Waking up every slumbering solitude,
   And sending out, with never-ceasing flow,
A different strain on the wings of every breeze,
   Now loud, now soft, now rapid, and then slow,
      With many a merry change;
And causing men, for thy wild, wondrous range,
   Halt in their journeying, and seek to know
What emulous mad bird pours out a song so strange.

Thou small philosopher, who laughest at
   All troubles of the world! I would that I
Thy mirth and merriment could imitate,
   And high above all care and trouble fly.
Thou art not drunken with rich, rosy wine;
   Joy ever nestles in thy happy heart,
Shaking a dewy influence divine
   From his soft wings upon it. Thou, whose throat
Surpasses in its powers all human art,
   Who startlest each lone bird with his own note,
      As if thou wert his mate;—
Thou, whose fine song is heard, early and late,
   Through the thick leaves and flowers to dance and float;—
Teach me the joyful secret of thy happy state!

It can not be that thou, who now dost sing
  With so tumultuous melody, while round
All spirits of the woods are hovering
  And drinking in with eager ears each sound,—
It can not be that thou, too, dost conceal
  The sorrows of thy soul in stormy mirth,
Or that thou dost not in good earnest feel
  The joyance of thy song. That is for men
Who walk alone on the pain-peopled earth,
  And pour out melodies with tongue and pen
      That all the world admire;
While they with their own songs grow faint and tire,
  And sadly droop and languish, even when
Their golden verse burns brightest with poetic fire.

1828.

ORA ATQUE LABORA.
PRAY AND WORK

Swiftly flashing, hoarsely dashing,
Onward rolls the mighty river;
   Down it hurries to the sea,
   Bounding on exultingly;
Still the lesson teaching ever,
   ORA ATQUE LABORA!

Trembling fountains on blue mountains,
Murmuring and overflowing,
   Through green valleys deep in hills,
   Send down silver brooks and rills;
Singing, while in sunlight glowing,
   ORA ATQUE LABORA!

Onward flowing, ever growing,
In its beauty each rejoices;
   While on Night's delighted ear,
   Through the amber atmosphere,
Sounds the murmur of their voices,
   ORA ATQUE LABORA!

Archly glancing, lightly dancing,
See its eddies chase each other;
 Round old roots they flashing whirl,
 Over ringing pebbles curl;
Each one singing to his brother,
 ORA ATQUE LABORA!

Still descending, mingling, blending,
Lo! a broad, majestic river!
 Under whose perpetual shocks,
 Lofty crags and columned rocks
Shaken, echo as they quiver,
 ORA ATQUE LABORA!

Hoarsely roaring, swiftly pouring
Through tall mountains cloven asunder,
 Over precipices steep,
 Plunging to abysses deep,
Loud the cataract's voices thunder,
 ORA ATQUE LABORA!

Sunlight shifting, white mist drifting
On its forehead, thence it marches,
   Swelled with freshets and great rains,
   Shouting through the fertile plains,
Spanned with aqueducts and arches,
   ORA ATQUE LABORA!

Thus Endeavour striveth ever
For the thankless world's improvement;—
   Each true thought and noble word,
   By the dull earth, though unheard,
Making part of one great movement,—
   ORA ATQUE LABORA!

Work then bravely, sternly, gravely,—
Life for this alone is given;
   What is right, that boldly do,
   Frankly speak out what is true,—
Leaving the result to Heaven,
   ORA ATQUE LABORA!

1844.

BROWN OCTOBER.

October, brown October, with his slow
   And melancholy step, has left the hills
And comes upon the plains. The wild winds blow
   Through the thick leaves, with cold and gusty thrills,
Turning their greenness to the sere red hues
   Of sober Autumn. Through the murmuring dells,
Heralded by the frost, that wildly strews
      The faded leaves along his way, strides on
The sober Month: and over the bright eye
      Of the desponding sun,
      The cold clouds fold their vesture dun,
Or on the bare gray hills like couching eagles lie.

The crimson heart of every summer flower
   Has pined away; and round the withered stalks
The gray and faded leaves begin to shower
   Into a rotting mass: uncertain flocks
Of winged seeds go floating through the air,
   Steered by mad winds: struck by the noiseless shocks
Of the white frost, the long night busy there,
      The nuts bestrew the ground. Fields mourn the loss
Of verdure; and the stubble, dry and gray,
      That the chill wind-gusts toss,
      While the dun clouds drift thick across,
Seems, with a useless life, to sadly waste away.

How well the time accordeth with the soul!

   Autumn is in the heart: and these sere woods,
These winds that coldly through the valley roll,

   These dull blue clouds, these withered solitudes,
Gray weeds and falling leaves, do all resemble

   The lonely season on the soul that broods:
The winds of sorrow through its pale blights tremble,

     Its falling hopes and passions in decay,
Like the dead leaves, give melancholy warning,

     That life ebbs fast away

     From the sad heart, once glad and gay
With the unsullied greenness of its life's young morning.

And now, oh Life! it makes its calm farewell!

   No peace or joy it hopeth for on earth,
The crimson fountain once did gladly swell,

   But now it hardly throbs. The jocund mirth
Of boyhood's day has gone, and in its stead

   Sit Weariness, and Loneliness, and Dearth:
The golden visions from the soul have fled,

     And each has left a sombre shadow there,
Amid which memory sees the once-loved faces,

     And in the whispering air

     Hears soft, voices say, "Prepare,
O weary one, to leave the old and well-known places."

                       1832.

TAOS.

The light of morning now begins to thrill
    Upon the purple mountains, and the gray
Mist-robed old pines. Brightly upon the still
    Deep banks of snow looks out the eye of Day;—
    The constant stream runs plashing on its way,
As melted stars might flow along blue heaven,
    And its white foam grows whiter, with the play
Of sunlight, down its rocky channel driven,
Like the eternal splendor from God's forehead given.

And tree, rock, pine, all are enveloped now
    With light, as with a visible soul of love:
Down the rough mountain sides the breezes blow,
    And in and out each grassy shaded cove,
    Making the scared dark from its dens remove,
To pine away amid the splendor-shower
    That raineth to the depths of each dim grove,
And under all the rocks that sternly lower,
And even in the caves and jagged grots doth pour.

Yet a small cloud goes wandering here and there,
    Whose only care seems up the hill to float,
Until the sun be risen broad and fair;
    And then the unseen angel that takes note
    To steer in safety this ethereal boat,

Will turn its helm toward heaven's untroubled seas,
   Where its white sail will glimmer, like a mote,
One moment, and then vanish. Now the trees
Through it are seen, like shadows through transparencies.

Now the sweet dew from the rich flower-bells,
   And from the quivering blades of bended grass,
Begins to rise invisibly, and swells
   Into the air,—the valley's humble mass;
   Like the rich incense that to God doth pass
Out of the bruised heart: the cricket's hymn,
   The bird's glad anthem, the cicada's bass,
All people with their influence the dim
Soul's·solitude, in this most brief, sweet interim.

Now Sorrow, sitting quietly and still,
   With look all gentle, and with sad smiles kind,
And sharing in all nature's joyous thrill,
   Breathes a delicious influence on the mind,
   A soothing melancholy, hope-inclined;
Like the faint memory of a painful dream,
   At which the heart once wept itself stone-blind;
But now which doth part pain part pleasure seem,
Until we know not which the feeling most to deem.

But soon will Sorrow re-subject her own,
   Although this golden and delicious calm

Hath shaken her in her accustomed throne;
    Although she sleeps, like Peace, with open palm,
    And quiet eyelid, and relaxed arm.
Soon Memory again will learn to sting,
    Recovered from this most unusual charm,
And from the past will gather up, and bring
Into the heart sharp agonies, its cords to wring.

She will point back to home and hearth forsaken,
    To friends grown cold, perhaps inimical;
And Love again will shudderingly awaken
    From troubled slumber; poverty enthrall,
    And shroud again, with dark and icy pall,
My hopes, my happiness, my fatherland;
    And I once more shall stand amid them all,
Cast them aside with rash and hasty hand,
Shiver my household gods, and 'mid the ruins stand.

Beloved New England! whom these jagged rocks,
    These chanting pines, this sea of snowy light,
These mountains, lifted by volcanic shocks,
    And now defying them; this hoarded white
    Of snows, that scoffs at the sun; this vale so bright,
And all the thousand objects here in view,
    Bring brightly forward into memory's sight
Thy hills, thy dells, thy streams thy ocean blue,
Thy gorgeous sky, and clouds of so surpassing hue.

I have gone from thee, and perhaps forever,
>Land of the free, the beautiful, the brave!
It was a mournful hour which saw me sever
>The ties that bound me unto thee; which gave
>Me living unto exile's narrow grave;
And now my heart is all, ay, all thine own:
>Again above me thy old forests wave,
Again I hear the Atlantic's deep grave tone;
I live with thee, and am even in the world alone.

Wherever I may roam, I shall be proud
>Of thee, old mother! and no less of thine:
Thy knee hath never to a tyrant bowed,
>Thou hast allowed no heresies to twine
>Around thee, as the gaudy poison-vine
Twines round the oak, and rots it to its core;
>I love thee, and my heart is ever thine:
And here, alone, I think of thee the more,
And pace these flinty hills, and on thy glories pore.

For here, beneath these mountain-summits gray,
>I think of those old venerable aisles,
Where I have passed on many a holy day,
>Into the sanctity of ancient piles,
>To hear thy sober creed; of those green isles

149

That gem thy bays and quiet ocean-nooks;
    Of the bright eyes and cheeks enwreathed with smiles,
That make thee famous: of still lakes and brooks;
And, more than all, I think of quietude and books.

What is there left, that I should cling to life?
    High hopes that storms smote down when scarce ex-
        panded;
A broken censer with faint odor rife,—
    A waning sun,—a vessel half-ensanded,—
    Life's prospects on sharp rocks and shallows stranded,—
A star just setting in a midnight ocean,—
    A smoking altar, broken and unbanded,—
Lit with the flame of hopeless love's devotion,—
A bosom shattered with its own intense emotion.

Unmanly heart! Repine not, but be calm!
    Take courage, Heart! Let us not madly mar
The effect of this sweet scene. Hope holds her palm,
    Like an old friend, to me, and sets her star
    Once more upon the waves of life afar;
It shall not sink again; but ever lift
    Cheerily its eye above the stormy bar.
I thank thee, Hope, for thy most princely gift!
No longer, eyeless, on life's clashing waves I drift.

Farewell to thee, New England! Once again
    The echo of thy name has reached my soul,
And it has vibrated: oh, not in vain,
    If thou and thine shall hear. Now for the goal!
    Dash through the waves, bold Heart, that madly roll
Across thy path! Much waiteth to be done,
    Before Time's billows o'er my dead brain roll:
Behold the last complaining words of one,
Who has been, is, will ever be, New England's son.

1832.

SUNSET IN ARKANSAS.

Sunset again! Behind the massy green
  Of the continuous oaks the sun hath fallen,
And his last rays have struggled through, between
The leaf-robed branches, as hopes intervene
  Amid gray cares. The western sky is wallen
  With shadowy mountains, built upon the marge
Of the horizon, from Eve's purple sheen,
And thin, gray clouds, that insolently lean
  Their silver cones upon the crimson verge
Of the high Zenith, while their unseen base
  Is rocked by lightning. It will show its eye
When dusky Night comes. Eastward, you can trace
  No stain, no spot of cloud upon a sky,
    Pure as an angel's brow.
  The winds have folded up their swift wings now,
And, all asleep, high up in their cloud-cradles lie.

Beneath the trees, the dusky, purple glooms
  Are growing deeper, more material,
In windless solitude. The young flower-blooms
Richly exhale their thin invisible plumes
  Of odor, which they yield not at the call
  Of the hot sun. The birds all sleep within

152

SUNSET IN ARKANSAS.

"He treads the West, and sends in glittering crowds
  His flocks of colors forth upon the river
Of the blue sky, there spirit-like to cling
To the cloud-cliffs and waves, there wandering
  And circling westwardly the world forever."

Unshaken nests; save the gray owl, that booms
His plaintive cry, like one that mourns strange dooms;
   And the sad whip-poor-will, with lonely din.
There is a deep, calm beauty all around,
   A heavy, massive, melancholy look,
A unison of lonely sight and sound,
      Which touch us, till the soul can hardly brook
         Its own sad feelings here.
   They do not wring from the full heart a tear,
But give us heavy thoughts, like reading a sad book.

Not such thy sunsets, oh New England! Thou
   Hast more wild grandeur in thy noble eye,
More majesty upon thy rugged brow.
When Sunset pours on thee his May-time glow,
   He looks on capes and promontories high,
   Gray granite mountain, rock and precipice,
Crowned with the white wreaths of the long-lived snow;
On sober glades, and meadows wide and low;
   On wild old woods, gloomy with mysteries;
On cultivated fields, hedged with mossed rocks,
   And greening with the husbandman's young treasure;
On azure ocean, foaming with fierce shocks
   Against stout shores, that his dominion measure;
      On towns and villages,
And environs wealthy with flowers and trees,
Full of gray, pleasant shades, and sacred to calm leisure.

When Sunset radiantly unfolds his wing
   Upon thy occident, and fills the clouds
With his rich spirit, while the laughing Spring
Leans towards the arms of Summer, like a king
   He treads the West, and sends in glittering crowds
   His flocks of colors forth upon the river
Of the blue sky, there spirit-like to cling
To the cloud-cliffs and waves, there wandering
   And circling westwardly the world for ever.
Thy sunsets are more brilliant and intense
   But not so melancholy or so calm,
As this that now is fast retreating hence,
   Shading his heavy eyes with misty palm,
     Lulled to an early sleep
   By Thunder, from the western twilight's deep,
Under the far horizon muttering a stern psalm.

1833.

WHEN CALIFORNIA WAS A FOREIGN LAND.

Read Before the National Convention of Mexican War
Veterans, January 16, 1874.

"When California was a foreign land!"
How many shadowy, ghost-like figures stand
Between that Then and Now!—forms of dead Years,
Old, meager, pale; and four all blood and tears,
With faces full of pain and agony,
And sitting bowed in speechless misery:
And three, the farthest from us, laurel-crowned,
The Years for victories over foreign foes renowned.

Comrades and Friends, the glorious Past recall;
Live in it again; in memory upon all
Your well-known fields of battle stand again,
Young, hopeful, eager, proud, as you were then.—
Rebels, against the tyranny of time,
Ride through the hills, the mountain-passes climb;
Camp on the streams through fertile vales that flow,
From the broad beds of everlasting snow;
Hear once again the Aztec eagle scream;
See once again Santana's lances gleam;
The toils and hardships of the march endure;
Win glory, and your country's thanks secure.

"WHEN CALIFORNIA WAS A FOREIGN LAND!"—
If time's not measured by the dropping sand
That counts the silent moments as they flit,
But by the great deeds that are done in it,
Then, Comrades, 't is a century or more
Since Yankee arms the flag of glory bore,
From Palo Alto, and from Vera Cruz,
Destined the day upon no field to lose,
To the Belen gate; and on its every fold
To have new glories added to the old;—
By Taylor's legions won at Monterey;
On Buena Vista's memorable day;
Where Kearney led to victory his command,
And Stockton's sailors learned to fight on land;
At Sacramento, where the brave troops, led
By Doniphan, the foe discomfited;
On Churubusco's bloody causeway won;
By deeds of valor at Contreras done;
When Worth and Quitman stormed Chapultepec,
And Mexico lay stranded like a wreck.

After Resaca, when the Motherland,
With sword uplifted in her mighty hand,
Called on her sons to meet the braggart foe,
And bear her banners into Mexico,
Her trumpet-call, in every hamlet heard,
The North and South alike inspired and stirred,

Then from the icy hills of pine-clad Maine,
And the great lakes, rang out the same refrain,
To the Mexique Gulf and farthest Arkansas—
"Ready!" and "Forward to the seat of war!"
Then from the cities reigning by the sea,
And inland marts of earnest industry,
From the lone homes of hardy husbandmen,
Came forth the toilers with the plow and pen,
Idlers and artisans, to volunteer;
To all alike their country's honor dear.
Little they cared the cause of war to know;
Enough for them that far in Mexico,
Our little army, then the nation's pride,
Faced gallantly red war's advancing tide,
And if not shortly re-inforced would be,
It and the nation's flag, in jeopardy:—
The flag that tyranny abhors and hates,
Whose golden Stars the symbols were of States,
Each star a sun that with its own light shone,
Not planets, with reflected light alone,—
And making with their stellar harmony
The Constellation's radiant unity.

Then, one by one, the days of glory came,
That neither North nor South alone could claim,
Nor wished to; whose immortal memories are
The common heritage of every Star;

Until the conquest of a nation crowned
Our arms, and golden California found
No tyrant, by the right of conquest Lord,
To rule her by the tenure of the sword;
But Freedom, ruling by her right divine,
Making her, too, a Star, with ours to shine.
Nor did we take her by the sword alone,
But by fair purchase made her all our own.

England remembers with no lessening pride,
The old fields by her sons' blood sanctified;
Remembers Agincourt, and Crecy, too,
And Poictiers, as well as Waterloo.
Shall the old glories of OUR arms grow pale,
Eclipsed by the latter? Shall the names grow stale,
And dim, like stars veiled by an envious cloud,
Of which their country once was justly proud?
Let US, at least, in reverence hold these names,
And guard with jealousy their worthy fames;
Honoring, as then we honored, all the brave,
When Illinois strewed flowers on Butler's grave,
When Indiana mourned the fate of Yell,
And Mississippi wept when Hardin fell;
Remembering that we all were Yankees there,
And in the common glory had a share,
Consenting not that any State should claim
Exclusive right to any hero's fame.

AUTUMN.

It is the evening of a pleasant day,
  In these old woods. The sun profusely flings
His golden light through every narrow way
    That winds among the trees: His spirit clings
    In orange mist around the snowy wings
Of many a patient cloud that now, since noon,
  Over the western mountain idly swings,
Waiting, when night-shades come, alas! too soon,
  To veil the timid blushes of the virgin moon.

The trees with crimson robes are garmented,
  Clad with frail brilliance by the wrinkling frost;
For the young leaves that Spring with beauty fed,
  Their greenness and luxuriance have lost,
  Gaining new beauty at too dear a cost,—
Unnatural beauty, essence of decay.
  Too soon, upon the harsh winds wildly tossed,
Leaving the naked trees ghost-like and gray,
  These leaf-flocks, like vain hopes, will vanish quite away.

159

How does your sad, yet calm, contented guise,
　　Ye melancholy autumn solitudes!
With my own feelings softly harmonize;
　　For though I love the hoar and solemn woods,
　　In all their manifold and changing moods,
In gloom and sunshine, storm and quietness,
　　By day, and when the dim night on them broods,
Their lightsome glades, their deep, dark mysteries,
　　Yet a sad heart best loves a still, calm scene like this.

Soon will the year, like this sweet day, have fled
　　With swift feet speeding noiselessly and fast,
As a ghost speeds to join its kindred dead,
　　In the dark realms of that mysterious Vast,
　　The shadow-peopled, vague and infinite PAST.
Life's current downward flows, a rapid stream,
　　With clouds and shadows often overcast,
Yet lighted by full many a sunny beam,
　　Of happiness, like sweet thoughts in a gloomy dream.

Like the brown leaves our loved ones drop away,
   One after one, into the dark abyss
Of sleep and death; the frosts of trouble lay
   Their withering touch upon our happiness,
   Even as the hoar-frosts of the Autumn kiss
The green life from the unoffending leaves;
   And Love, and Hope, and Youth's warm cheerfulness,
Flit from the heart;—Age lonely sits and grieves,
   Or sadly smiles, while Youth his day-dream fondly weaves.

Day draweth to its close: Night cometh on:
   Death, a dim shape, stands on Life's western verge,
Casting his shadow on the startled sun,
   A deeper gloom that seemeth to emerge
   From endless night. Forward he bends, to urge
His eyeless steeds, fleet as the tempest's blast;
   Hark! hear we not Eternity's grave surge,
Thundering anear? At the dread sound aghast,
   Time, pale with frantic terror, hurries headlong past.

1842.

THE STRUGGLE FOR FREEDOM.

The Ancient Wrong rules many a land, whose groans
　　Rise swarming to the stars by day and night,
Thronging with mournful clamour round the thrones
　　Where the Archangels sit in God's great light,
And, pitying, mourn to see that Wrong still reigns,
　　And tortured Nations writhe in galling chains.

From Hungary and France fierce cries go up
　　And beat against the portals of the skies;
Lashed Italy still drinks the bitter cup,
　　And Germany in abject stupor lies;
The knout on Poland's bloody shoulder rings,
　　And Time is all one jubilee of kings.

It will not be so always.　Through the night
　　The suffering multitudes with joy descry
Beyond the ocean a great beacon-light,
　　Flashing its rays into their starless sky,
And teaching them to struggle and be free,—
　　The light of Order, Law, and Liberty.

Take heart, ye bleeding Nations; and your chains
   Shall shiver like thin glass. The dawn is near,
When Earth shall feel, through all her aged veins
   The new blood pouring; and her drowsy ear
Hear Freedom's trumpet ringing in the sky,
   Calling her braves to conquer or to die.

Arm and revolt, and let the hunted stags
   Against the lordly lions stand at bay!—
Each pass, Thermopylæ, and all the crags,
   Young Freedom's fortresses!—and soon the day
Shall come when Right shall rule, and round the thrones
   That gird God's feet shall eddy no more groans.

                                        1853.

FANTASMA.

I sit, unconscious of all things around,
And look into my soul. Within it far
There is an image, dim and indistinct.
Of something that hath been,—I know not which,—
A dream or a reality. In vain
I strive to force it assume a visible shape,
And be condensed to thought and memory.
At times I catch a glimpse of it, behind
The clouds and shadows weltering in the chasm
Of the deep soul; and when I seem to grasp
The half-embodied echo of the dream,
When it hath almost grown an audible sound,
Then it retreats, seeking the inner caverns.
And undisturbed recesses of the mind,—
Recesses yet unpeopled by quick Thought,
Or Conscience, Hope, Love, Fear or Memory;—
And there it hides. Now, while I separate
Myself yet more from my external life,
And look within, I see the floating thoughts,
Quiver amid the chaos of the soul;
And slowly they assume a more distinct
And palpable appearance. One by one,
Dimly, like shadows upon ocean waves,
For a brief moment they are memory.

164

I see a boy, reading at deep, dead night:
The lamp illuminates his pallid face,
Through the thin hand which shades his deep black eyes,
Half-bedded in the clustering, damp, dark hair.
He closes up the book, and rising takes
A step or two;—and now I hear him speak
Unto himself, in low and murmuring tones:
"The fountain is unsealed. This ancient rhyme
Has shown my heart to me, and waked the tide
Of poetry that slept within the soul.
Now do I know my fate. The latent love,
At length revealed, of wild and burning song,
Will make me wretched. Never, until now,
Knew I the wish and bent of my own mind;
And now I look into it as a new
And inexhaustible treasure. Burning words,
Wild feelings, broken hopes, await me now.
If I win fame, ever unsatisfied,
If not, life's spring and summer gone in vain.
Ah! what a woe were gift of prophecy,
And foresight of the future! What one soul,
Knowing what waits it, could exist, and bear
The agonies that knowledge would create?
And yet, ah me! this gift of Pandora
Must be received, and Destiny have its way;
Though the heart, shivering all its idols, sit
Lonely and desolate and comfortless

In a great desert, peopled only with
Gray-headed hopes, and memories of joys
Dead long ago, and buried many years:
Though in its desolation the sad soul
Be like a house deserted, with the doors
And windows open to the winter wind,
The lamps extinct, cold moonlight shining in,
Through shattered casements and wind-shivered blinds,
With haggard eye. So, Destiny, have thy way!"—
I see him hide his face within his hands:—
Was it to weep? It might be. He was young,
And tears fall freely in the spring of life.
In after years the brain becomes more dry,
The springs of the heart sink deeper, or, perhaps,
Choked up and more obstructed. He was young,
And had not known the bent of his own mind,
Until the mighty spells of COLERIDGE woke
Its faculties, as did the wondrous staff
Of God's own prophet, the sealed desert-rock.
He felt his fate: he knew that to a mind
Enthusiastic, wayward, shy as his,
Poetry would shape out an ideal world,
Living in which, he would become unfit
For this, our every-day and human life,
Unfit to struggle and to jostle with
The busy, selfish world; among the crowd,
Earning the pittance of a livelihood.

He did not know how, in new scenes, and lands
Remote in the west, even such a soul, compelled
To measure itself with others, and to wage
Industrious battle against circumstance,
Grows stout and strong, with energetic strength
And self-relying vigor, as the hands
Grow larger and robuster with long toil.
He knew not this and wept. It was not strange.

That shadow vanishes; and like a man,
That on the shore of a great weltering sea
Stands gazing dreamily acróss its waves,
To the distant indistinctness, I behold
Another shadow gathering in the chamber,
Where dwell old dreams and antenatal echoes:
And now its images, like thoughts, take shape.
I see the boy sit in a crowded room:
His eyes have still that melancholy look,
His cheek and brow are pale; his wasted form
Tells of long hours of study, and of lamps
Burned beyond midnight. Bright eyes smile upon him,
That might make summer in a wintry heart;
Transparent cheeks are flushed, when his sad voice
Murmurs soft words, soft as of one at night
Holding communion with himself; for Praise
Has fed his eager spirit with her rain
Of dangerous sweetness. Songs of wild and stern

167

And energetic import, or low, sweet
Æolic tones, have in a few months gained
A name for the enthusiastic boy.
He, with the same intense and constant look
With which the eye looks inward on the soul,
And with a deep expression of devotion,
Gazes intensely on a single face.
She knows not of his love; yet cautiously
Steals looks at him, and seems to him more cold,
Because she loves him. For he has not told '
His love, even when from his tumultuous heart
Passion has overflowed, and he has uttered
His feelings to the world. This rapturous one
He has kept hidden in his inmost soul,
Like a delicious and yet poisonous dew.
For only when the passions have by time
Lost some intensity, and grown more calm,
They shape themselves, in rhyme and measured verse.
After a time it is a sad relief,
To weigh and ponder sorrow every way,
To view it in all lights, and thus to weave
Passion and sadness into poetry.
I lose the shadow. Will its place be filled?
Dark, darker yet grows the chaotic vast.
And now it seems a sea, with clouds above
That purple its dark waters, where they stretch
Far off towards unknown continents of mist,

Looming mysteriously along its edge,
On the grim surface of that dead sea moves
The half-embodied spirit of a dream,
Like an unshapen dread upon the soul,
A heavy fear, which has no visible cause.
When will the dream rise upward from the chasm,
And be revealed? Oh, when? I can not yet
Express it to myself. The darkness now
Quivers like clouds by sudden lightning shaken;
And now more clearly I behold the dream:
I see the youth stand in a crowded street;
The shade of manhood is upon his lip,
His thin form has grown thinner, his dark eye
Speaks of a sharper and more urgent pain;
No muscle quivers in his stern, pale face,
His brow contracts not, though its swelling veins
Throb strongly under the transparent skin.
With downcast eyes immovably he leans
Against a pillar of a haughty house,
Holding no converse with the crowd, that flows
With steady current past him; but his eyes
Look inward, pitying his wounded soul.
Another shadow rises. Ah, it is
The lady of his love! I see her pass
Close by the youth; and as she passes him,
He, by the sympathy that doth connect
His soul with hers, raises his sad, dark eyes.

They meet his idol's look. His pallid face
Is flushed with pain, his slight frame shaken with
A quick, sharp agony, great beads of sweat
Start on his forehead, and his thin pale lips,
As if they strove to speak to a spirit, parting,
Utter a stifled, incoherent sound.
One mute, sad gesture is his last farewell.
The frost of poverty has frozen his hopes,
Withering their rainbow wings, as northern snows
Wither the Arabian jasmine's delicate blooms.
Weary of fruitless toil, he leaves his home,
To seek in other climes a fairer fate,
Which he will yet accomplish; for his soul
Will every day by adversity gain strength
To do with vigor his appointed task.
He leaves his home; henceforth, at least for a time,
To wander like a withered, fallen leaf,
Borne idly by the currents of the air,
Or tossing unregarded on the waves;
Himself a wave of the universal ocean,
Bearing a star within its heart of love.
Gone like the spirit of an echo! Gone
Into the deep recesses of the soul!
But still the lamp of one white, glittering star
Lights up the dim abyss of memory.
Another shadow rises, under which
The wild, chaotic darkness waits, to whelm

170

It like the other dreams. I see a desert,
And thereupon our youth, now grown a man.
Great changes have been wrought upon his soul:
His sorrows still are there; but kindly now,
Like ancient friends, they people his strong heart.
Like shadows round the roots of sturdy trees,
Feeding them with an influence of love,
They have fed his soul, and made its pulses calm.
He has communed with nature, in her moods
Of stern and silent grandeur, and of sweet
And still content, of calm and frantic storm,
Among the peaks of mighty mountains, and
Upon the plains these Titans ever guard,
Like sleepless and untiring sentinels.
Alone with nature, he has there communed
Most intimately with his soul, and traced
Its deep thought-fountains to their hidden source.
He is prepared to battle with the world,
And force his upward way through the wild surge
That swelters over him, and through the drift
That floats and eddies on the tossing tide.
Now stout of soul, and strong to dare and do,
He is prepared to hew himself a path
To fame and fortune; a firm-hearted man,
A full-grown energetic man; and now
No longer an enthusiastic boy,
Bending to every rough blast from the sky:

A lover still of all the beautiful,
And more than all, of one sweet pitying face
That comes to him in dreams, and even by day
Looks in his eyes and loves him more and more.
This is his nature.

I lose the dream. Again the purple clouds
Throng from the void, and fill the darkened soul.
The glittering star of memory fades away:
The echoes ring no longer on the sea
Of dreams and dead realities.

                              Remember,
And lay to heart, ye young and ardent souls,
This lesson of a wayward, passionate youth,
Whom, almost ruined by the faithless tide
Of his own morbid feelings, solitude
And loneliness and labor have preserved!
Repine not, if ye have been borne to toil
With poverty, and grieve for shattered hopes!
Gird up yourselves, and like good men and true,
Do manfully whatever is to do!
Front storm and tempest boldly, march straight on
In your determined path, and from the world
You shall force fame and fortune, and find new
And faithful friends to fill the places of the old.
Bright eyes and warm hearts every where are found;

    And while life lasts 'tis folly to despair,
Work then! work steadily on! Reward will come at last.

                                                1833.

MONOTONE.

Come, gentle Dian, show thy crescent in
The sea of fading light that floods the west:
Sit, like a white swan on a blue sea's breast;
A dying swan, that with sweet melody
Of her last song tames the rebellious sea,
To slumberous quiet. Oh, shine forth, amid
The paling light, like beauty's lovely eye,
Half-beaming from its slowly lifting lid!
Shine out, and bless the world, fair Moon! for I,
Like the young flowers and leaves, do watch for thee,
As though thou wert the pleasant memory
Of a lost happiness.

           I see her now,
And my heart quivers with a sudden glow
Of soothing sadness; as the still leaves move,
When the breeze stirs them with his voice of love.
Oh, gentle Moon! thy influence is like
A mother's love, thy light, a mother's eye.
Ah, mother, mother! how that dear name sends

Its echoes through the heart, and with them blends
The keen, fierce intonations of sharp woe!
Mother, dear mother! dark and sad is now
My path of life; heart-stricken and alone,
We tread our way in joyless unison.

Those that we love so dearly, all are gone:
All, all are dead: and, mother, sadly thou
Thinkest of me, and weepest for thy son,
Toiling afar with the wild waves of life,
Stricken with tempest.   Shall I ever steer
Homeward my shattered bark, and once more hear
Thy kind, calm tones of love, and feel thine eye
Beaming with deep affection, and the high
And holy spirit of a mother's love?
Yet even then how changed, how sad and stern
Will be my home, when anxiously I turn
Mine eyes around, to search for each lost face
That there should greet me!

> Time, thy ceaseless pace
Tramples the heart and all its growth of hopes,

Like withering flowers.   Go on, cold reveller!
And end thy work!   I have had dreams, fond dreams,
Bright hopes, wild, fiery graspings after fame,
Flashes of proud ambition in my heart,
But all are buried now in many graves.
For what were home to me, should I return?
A trampled hearth, whose fire has ceased to burn!
A silent desert! a monotony!
A voiceless echo! an unshapen void,
Lighted by one pale star! ah, bitter thought,
Perhaps all starless!   Mother! can it be,
That I shall lose thee, too? the fearful thought
Crushes my soul.   All?   All?—Oh, spare me one!
Leave me one eye of love to light my soul,
When I return!

1834.

THE FIRST WILD-FLOWER OF SPRING.

Young nursling of the Spring and southern wind!
  Thou comest like tenderness fostered by neglect,
Or like new hope within a desert mind,
  Lonely and beautiful. With new gladness decked,

The Earth is waking from her dreamless sleep
  Of barrenness and winter. Warmer airs
Come hovering down from the great upper Deep,
  And brood upon her. The wide azure wears

The semblance of a sleeping ocean, in
  Its great blue eye, and wandering clouds spread out
Upon that upper sea their canvas thin,
  And float, obedient to the winds, about

Over its depths, freighted with rain and dew,
Wherewith to bless the trees and struggling flowers,
When Night, in pensive silence, wanders through
The clustering stars, guarded by darkling hours.

Spring, gentle Spring! thou nurse of happiness!
  Cradled at first among cold winter winds,
And thronging clouds, gloomy and motionless!
  Thou comest like a dream of joy, that blinds

The heart with happiness; and thou dost bless
   The barren earth, and the deep sluggish minds
Of men benumbed by winter. The glad ocean
Lifts his blue waves to thee, with deep emotion.

Aye! thou didst sleep, while Winter ruled, afar,
   In the calm greenness of the sea-girt isles;
While every wondering and impatient star
   Watched for the coming of thy many smiles,
And thy soft winds, that would the frosts unbar,
   Whereby the seed-girt flowers were held in piles
Of frozen earth. Yet still thy sleep was calm,
Beneath the olive and the graceful palm.

Then thou didst wake; thy genial influence poured
   From the unmeasured crystalline of heaven;
The winds of winter fled away, and roared
   Behind the western mountains; life was given
To the earth again; the quiet rains were showered
   On its cold brow; its frozen mass was riven,
And like wakening dreams, the flowers sprang up,
Each holding to the sun its thirsty cup

One sprang, as suddenly as first love springs
   At times, within the lonely soul, from out
The mass of damp leaves and decaying things,
   And shyly looked at the sun, in timid doubt;

And then great clouds opened their snowy wings,
    And, eagle-like, sailed leisurely about,
So that the light rain and the lighter dew
Fell, like a spiritual influence, through

The chasm of air. The joyful earth vibrated;
    Verdure shot up, like many a pleasant thought
Of universal joy; the sea, elated,
    Quaked on his shores; with melody untaught,
The birds sang loud; and everything created
    A new joy from the Spring's young spirit caught:
And all, from man to the poor worm that crawls,
Felt like worn captives freed from Pagan thralls.

Spring, sweetest of the seasons! welcome here,
    As calm is to the storm-tossed mariner,
Wine to the goblet, music to the ear,
    Thou to the poet art,—aye! welcomer.
When Summer heralds thee unto thy bier,
    As Autumn in his turn shall herald her,
Thy memory to me shall yet be sweet,
As of loved friends whom still we hope to meet.

But thou, the earliest of the young Spring's dreams,
    Too early cam'st, and met'st the sharp white frost;
Lured by the Syren-song of babbling streams,
    Venturing too soon, to thy most bitter cost.

178

The chill east wind thy tender petals froze,
    And shy and pale thou nestlest quite away
Among thick leaves, and where the tall grass grows;—
    Thou hast arisen like a starry ray

Of sudden thought within a poet's brain,
    Or a swift flash of passionate love within
The soul of woman; and dost maintain
    Thyself aloof from the monotonous din

Of the old twirling oak leaves, from the moan
    Of the gray weeds, the dull monotony
Of the harsh winds, and the dead limb, that, lone
    And dry, swings creaking from the leafless tree.

Thou droopest toward the earth again, like one
    For life and its tumultuous storms unfit;
Now chilled and shivering; but the fiery sun,
    Like a great censer in the sky uplift,

Will shrivel soon thy slight leaves with his fire,
    And thou wilt vanish like a cloudy scroll;
As many a poet, fainting on his lyre,
    Wastes with the fiery passions of his soul.

1833.

A DIRGE.

OVER A COMPANION KILLED BY COMANCHES AND BURIED
IN THE PRAIRIE.

Thy wife shall wait
Many long days for thee;
And when the gate
Swings on its unused hinges, she,
Opening her dim and grief-contracted eye,
And still forbidding hope to die,
Longing for thee will look;
Till like some lone and gentle summer brook,
That pineth in the summer-heat away
And dies some day,
She waste her mournful life out at her eyes.
Vainly, ah! vainly we deplore
Thy death, departed friend! No more
Shalt thou be seen by us beneath the skies.
The barbed arrow has gone through
Thy heart, and all the blue
Hath faded from thy clay-cold veins, and thou,
With stern and pain-contracted brow,
Like one that wrestled mightily with death,
Art lying there.

180

Whether above the skies,
    Thou at thy death didst soar,
    And treadest Heaven's floor
With great joy beaming in thine eyes;
    Or buried there
    Commencest an eternal sleep,
And shalt in atoms only rise to the air,
    As thinks despair;—
We bid thee here a last, long, sad adieu!
    Rest there, pale sleeper!
    Another trophy of the grim old Reaper,
Cut down and withering under unknown skies.
Farewell! our course yet farther westward lies.
    Thy grave is deeper than the wolf can go,
    And we have driven the wheels above thee, so
That the Indian may not find thy sepulchre.
    Farewell! for now the trains begin to stir;
        And we with quivering lip,
        And lingering and reluctant step,
Must leave thee here, alone. Once more, farewell!

1832.

THE VOYAGE OF LIFE.

Our shallop, long with tempest tried,
Floats calmly down life's tranquil tide;
Blue skies are laughing overhead,
The river sparkles in its bed;
The sunbeams from the waters glancing,
On the white canvas flashing glisten;
The small waves round our vessel dancing,
  Melt and dissolve in silver foam,
  And we, in our frail home,
To the charmed water-music listen.

We and our little children float,
Dreaming, in this enchanted boat:
A gentle and propitious gale,
Follows, and fills the snowy sail,
From spicy Southern wildernesses,
And thickets of acacia blowing,—
Where dewy morning's golden tresses,
  Shine through the darkling purple gloom
  And, loaded with perfume,
The sea of air is overflowing.

182

Great trees their branches overhead
Thrust forth, with flowers thick-garlanded;
And while our little bark we steer
Through the bright rosy atmosphere,
  The thick leaves murmuringly quiver;
The golden sunlight, floating, flashes
  On green isles jewelling the river,
      On whose smooth, silver-sanded shore,
      Foaming up evermore,
The current musically plashes.

But westward a dark, frowning cloud
Veils the bright river, like a shroud;
Where, wandering under unknown skies,
  Its course is hidden from our eyes.
  We only know that onward ever,
Lapsing with fluctuating motion,
  The mighty and majestic river,
      To where the sunset glories fade,
      Through changing light and shade
Runs to Eternity's broad ocean.

Between what bleak and desert shores,
Down what harsh cataracts it pours,
Over what rocks and treacherous shoals,
The fretted river hoarsely rolls,
   We know not: We are in God's keeping:
He loves and will protect us ever.
   Now, while our little ones are sleeping,
      Kneel we in earnest prayer to Him
      To guide us through the dim
And unknown perils of Life's river.

THE DYING WIFE.

Dear husband, raise me in thine arms,—the hour is drawing
near
When I must part with thee, and these our little children
dear
Though froward often, I have been a loving, faithful wife,
And on thy breast I fain would rest, and breathe away my
life.

Nay, weep not! let me kiss the tears from thy dear eyes
away;—
They are dim with weary watching many a long sad night
and day:
It is our heavenly Father's will; I only go before
To that bright home, where we shall meet, to part again no
more.

The fresh world seems more beautiful, as life draws to its
close,
For death, like sunset, over it a mellow beauty throws.
All nature seems more lovely when life's day is nearly gone,
Than when it radiantly glowed, in childhood's rosy dawn.

How pleasantly the soft Spring sky is brightening again!
How cheerfully the meadows smile, after the sweet soft rain!
The waving corn-fields flash with light, like a forest of green
    spears,
And on the flowers, like jewels, shine the light rain's pearly
    tears.

The rustling leaves and pattering drops make music in the
    air,
The odor of the grateful flowers swells heavenward like a
    prayer,
The glad birds carol loudly, while they feed their happy
    young,
And the bees are very busy, leafy labyrinths among.

Soon will fair sunset's golden feet trample the western hill,
With crimson light ensandaled,—soon the busy world be
    still;
And long before the rosy morn wakes on the eastern sea,
Our little ones, dear husband, will be left alone with thee.

Alas, Alas! my children! Give me strength, dear God in
    Heaven!
Thou knowest how most earnestly and truly I have striven
To bow my heart submissively unto thy will divine;
Oh, Father, aid and strengthen me!—for I would not repine.

Now, husband, let me clasp them in a last, long sad embrace,
While yet my dim eyes can discern each sweet familiar face;
To-morrow they will wonder why their mother sleeps so still,
And why they can not wake her with sweet kisses at their will.

Farewell, dear children! Bitter tears are filling my tired
    eyes,—
I can not speak the thousand words, out of my heart that
    rise:
Your arms around your mother's neck no more will fondly
    twine,
Your sweet eyes, gazing into hers, no more with gladness
    shine.

She is going a long journey; many a Spring will come and
    go,—
To Summer heat and Autumn frosts succeed the Winter
    snow;
And still, from that far spirit-land, in which the bright stars
    burn,
No more, when daylight glads the earth, your mother will
    return.

But often, when, at night, your eyes are closed in gentle sleep,
She by each little pillow will a constant vigil keep;

And while the silver moonlight on each forehead softly
    streams,
She will visit all her little ones, and talk with them in
    dreams.

You must love your kind, good father; you must love each
    other well,
Nor ever say an angry word, nor any falsehood tell:
Be kind to everything that lives, and though I go before, ˙
You shall come to me in Heaven, and be with me evermore.

Dear husband, love our little ones, when I am dead and gone,
When the dewy grass and laughing flowers my grave are
    growing on;
Oh, cherish and protect them, lest they sadly pine away,
Like buds on which no longer shines the blessed light of day.

Thine eyes may fondly look upon some sweet girl's sunny
    face;
A fair young wife may sleep upon thy bosom in my place;
Other children may be born to thee, THY love with these
    to share,
But demanding and receiving ALL their youthful mother's
    care.

Yet these will be as dear to THEE; for in each little face,
The features of thy first love thou wilt still delight to trace:
I leave them, a rich legacy, beyond all price to thee,
And I know that thou wilt love them, for the love I bear to
    thee.

Slow sinks the sun,—the world grows dark,—dear husband,
    let us pray!
I am ready now resignedly to pass from earth away:
But a thought of thee, beloved, when all other thoughts
    depart,
Will linger yet, within the cold, dark chambers of the heart.

                      1840.

TO AMBITION.

Cry on! full well I know the voice,
　　For often it hath called on me,
Stirring my passions with the noise,
　　As tempests stir the hungering sea.
Cry on, ambition! 'tis in vain!
　　Thine influence hath passed away,
And mighty though thou art, again
　　Thou canst not bend me to thy sway.

Thou wakest dreams of fame and power;
　　Ha! I despise both thee and them;
They were illusions of an hour,
　　Mere shadows now, remote and dim;
I scorn them all: they wake no thrill
　　Within the heart where once they reigned
And revelled, and would revel still,
　　But smote by love, Ambition waned.

For what is fame, that man should pour
　　His life-blood for it, drop by drop;
And for a name, when life is o'er,
　　Drain to the dregs misfortune's cup?
Fame! 'tis the wrecker's light, that lures
　　The luckless wanderer of the deep,
To where, upon disastrous shores,
　　Ruin and wreck their vigils keep.

To waste away the burning heart,
    Pouring its bright thoughts on the sand
Of the regardless world; to part
    With mad and suicidal hand,
The ties that bind to life, and tread
    The desert of the world alone;
To leave no soul, when we are dead,
    Of grief for us to make one moan.

To be the mark for every base
    And slanderous miscreant's venomed tongue,
Hissed at by all the adder race,
    Their poison on my garments flung:
My fair name recklessly defiled
    With every crawling reptile's slime,
Slandered, belied, abused, reviled,
    Each action tortured into crime.

To fill the heart with scathing fire
    And bitter passions; to erase
The feelings holier and higher
    Which ruled there in our ealier days;
To make the soil a desert, burned
    And blasted with remorseless flame;
To be, at Life's best hour, inured
    Within this living death, called **Fame**:—

191

Will Fame, will Power, repay for this?
　　Cry on, then!—Even now I feel
The infant hands of happiness
　　Around my heart-strings gently steal,
And well I know that Fame has nought,
　　Or Power, to pay the sacrifice,
If with this happiness I bought
　　Their glorious uncertainties.

Give me Love's smile, my wife's fond eye,
　　To light the pathway of my life;
And vainly may Ambition cry,
　　And urge me to the stirring strife:
I would not sell my quiet home,
　　And those I love, for all the fame
Of all the mighty who entomb
　　Their sorrows in a splendid name.

1836.

HOME.

Though the heart hath been sunken in folly and guilt—
Though its hopes and its joys on the earth have been split—
Though its course hath become like the cataract's foam—
Still, still it is holy, when thinking on Home.

Though its tears have been shed like the rains of the spring—
Though it may have grown loath to existence to cling—
Oh, still a sweet thought like a shadow will come,
When the eye of the mind turns again to its Home.

Though the fire of the heart may have withered its core
Unto ashes and dust—though the head have turned hoar
Ere its time, as the surfs o'er the breakers that foam—
Still a tear will arise when we think upon Home.

1833.

THE DEAD CHASE.

A LEGEND.

A morning of early June,—
   The wind slept cradled in leaves,
And the throstles were singing a soft low tune,
   In the ivy under the eaves.

The silver brooklets murmured
   Sweet music in the grass;
As the faint tones of an organ
   Swell at the evening mass.

The velvet sward, like a smooth, green sea,
Glittered and flashed incessantly,
With dewy diamonds of the dawn,
Through which went springing the spotted fawn;
And the snake lay idly across the path,
That wound amid the vibrating swath.

Within the deep-green heavy glooms,
Were beds of orange and crimson blooms,
Whose sweet perfume and odor stole
To the inmost crypts of the grateful soul,
Like harmonies faintly heard, that seem
The sweet, sad memories of a dream.

The lily grew in the shade,
   And the dew-drop lay in its blossom,
Like a rosy diamond, laid
   On a virgin's snowy bosom:

The heart of the crimson rose was blushing
   At the kisses of the sun;
Like the cheek of a timid maiden, flushing
   After her heart is won.

A wall of cliffs half ringed the dell
   That sheltered by it slept;
In one gray crag a hollowed cell
Near which a leaping torrent fell,
   And a Hermit his vigils kept.

A snowy mountain, close behind,
   Shot upward like a flame,
From which with a roar like a mighty wind
   The headlong river came.

A man once proud and stately,
   Now haggard with despair;
Whose scared eyes, straining, seem to see
Far off some great calamity;
   Some terror, darkening all the air,
And armed with nameless agony.

The woodlark, from her low nest, toward
   The sky shot, like a dart,
Gladly carolling as she soared
   Into the sky's blue heart.

He neither heeds, nor hears, nor sees,
   Nature to him is dumb,
And all her charming coquetries
   Have odious become.

His face grows dark; no longer now
   His soul its dread obeys;
His eyes that full of anguish were,
   Like a hunted tiger's blaze.

A sound came clashing past,
   On the wings of the startled air,
Like the sound of hoofs that far and fast
   A reckless rider bear.

The eagle rose from the trackless snows,
   Where he sat like a king on his throne;
And high he flew, where the sunlight through
   His dark gray plumage shone;
Unfolded his heart in a wild scream there,
And fanned with his wings the morning air.

A great steed came, like a mighty rain,
   Down the steep mountain's side;
Thick as a storm his flowing mane,—
   A horse for a Prince to ride.
He stopped before the Hermit's cell,
Like a statue of stone, immovable.

And near this courser stood
A black hound, with fresh blood
   About his feet and upon his jaws;
His teeth were long, and sharp, and white,
Left by his curling lips in sight;
   His strong feet fanged with claws.

He bayed not, and he made no moan,
But beside the steed he sat like a stone,
   And looked in the Hermit's eye:
What want they with the Hermit,
   That on him thus they stare,—
That hound so fiery-eyed, that steed,
   A stern and silent pair?

The Hermit shuddered at the sight,
   But never a word he said;
Only his lips became as white
   As the marble lips of the dead.

Slowly he comes to the steed that waits,
    As men walk in their sleep;
As birds that a serpent fascinates
    Into their jaws do creep.

Now springs he upon the courser's back,
    Saddle and bridle none;
The hound has risen, and, baying loud,
    Down the green slope has gone.

Uprose the sun; the steed sped on;
    His hoofs the green sward tore;
Over stream and hill, through brake and dell,
    While the hound bayed on before.

He came to a river broad and deep;
Its waves ran high, its banks were steep;
    He made nor stop, nor stay,
But plunging in, through the loud din
    Of its rapids stretched away.

Over sharp rocks and hillsides bald,
    Where the spotted adder sleeps,—
Through forests as green as emerald,—
    As the tyrannous tempest sweeps,

All day, all day, he stretched away,
    And the tramp of his hoofs was heard,
Like an earthquake's foot, when his fiery heart
    In his adamant caves is stirred.

All day, all day, he stretched away,
    Till the gentle moon uprose,
And her soft, pale rays kissed Night's sweet face,
    The firs and the mountain-snows.

And then he was heard careering up
    That mountain's rocky side;
The eternal ice-crags crowned its top,
And the streams that poured from the Giant's cup,
    Rushed foaming down his side.

And now he follows the black sleuth-hound,
    On a glacier's frozen sea,
Grinding to snow with his iron hoof
Its still, green waves' transparent woof,
    That since God gave the world its form,
    Defies the lightning and the storm.

Midnight! midnight! The horse has stopped;
    The moon stands still, likewise;
Without a mist, without a cloud,
    The stars have shut their eyes.

The black hound circles round the steed:
  Loud baying,—long and loud;
The Hermit sits as pale as Death:
  But his eye is hard and proud.

A spectre comes athwart the moon;
  Her light gleams through its bones
A cold wind rushes swiftly by,
  All eddying with groans.

The mist of its long yellow hair
  Floats like a ragged cloud;
What does the skeleton, without
  A winding-sheet or shroud?

Out-springs the great black hound again;
  Once more the scent is won;
Leap after leap, bay after bay:
He and the horse stretch far away;—
  They chase the skeleton!

Day comes at last. The night is past,
  But still the hunt holds on;
On hound and horse and spectre shine
  The red rays of the sun.

Slow, slow as Death, Time draws his breath;
   'Tis a weary space to noon;
And high and high the sun's red eye
   Shines, shadowy, like the moon.

A desert stretches every way;
Dawn's crimson and dusk Evening's gray
   Rest upon either edge;
The wind above it sighs alway;
   Like the sighing of thin sedge.

In the middle of the desert
   The horse and hound have stopped;
The hunted skeleton, likewise:
   Upon the earth has dropped.

The hound lies panting by its side:
With his red nostrils open wide;
   His eyes like torches glare:
The rider too has left his steed:
   And sitteth speechless there.

Through his long hair the sharp wind moans:
   But all beside is still;
He can not choose but gaze upon
The green bones of the skeleton;
   Through which the breezes thrill.

All day they sat in the desert:
    Till the sun slid down the sky:
And in the west his lids of mist
    Were folded over his eye.

Then in the west a shape appeared:
    Between them and the sun;
Nearer and nearer yet it drew:
Until an armed man it grew:
    A mail-clad destrier on.

"What dost thou here with hound and horse:
    "Without a shield or spear?
"And why dost watch that skeleton:
    "So mossy, green, and sere?

"What dost thou here? Twilight draws near:
    "The weary Day recedes;
"Night's pilots her dark galley steer
"Among the trembling stars; while here
    "Thou tellest over thy beads:—

"What dost thou here?" "Alight and learn:
    " 'Tis long to mirk midnight:
"Another sun will set, before
    "Thou seest thy lady bright.

"Alight! I have a tale to tell:
   "It will profit thee to hear:—
"That will vibrate in thy memory
   "For many a long, long year."

   The Knight has leaped from his destrier,
      And sits by the Hermit's side,
   And listens to a strange, wild tale,
      There in the desert wide.

"A chase was held, long years ago,
   "On a sunny day of June,
"Where a hundred noble horsemen rode,
   "From morning till high noon,

"With wanton glee and revelry,
   "While the hounds before them ran;
"For, clad in steel, on strong, fleet steeds,
   "They chased an outlawed man.

"For many an hour we chased the game;
   "Hound after hound fell back,
"Till, man by man, I passed them all,
   "And my strong hound led the pack.

"All night led on the deep-mouthed hound;
  "And all night followed I;
"The wayward moon went slowly down,
  "The white stars left the sky.

"Uprose the sun; my hound kept on,
  "My good horse faltered not;
"And when the sun was in the south,
  "I reached this desert spot.

"The Heretic lay here. Ah, God!
  "That I that sight should see!
"His dead, dead eyes were opened wide,
  "And sadly gazed at me.

"His flesh was torn, his bones were bare,
  "All mangled was his head,
"And by his side my gaunt sleuth-hound
  "Lay, with his jaws blood-red.

"I sate down by the dead man's side;
  "I had no power to go;
"Methought that Time also was dead,
  "His feet went by so slow.

"My good hound fawned upon my breast,
"And kindly to him I caressed;
   "My tears did freely flow;
"I thought he was my only friend,
   "And God Himself my foe.

"Alas! that weary afternoon!
   "Nor sight nor sound came by;
"Only the lonesome wind, that through
   "The dead man's hair did sigh.

"The moon uprist, swathed in gray mist,
   "And up the heaven stole,
"While from the dead man's eyes, her light
   "Pierced to my inmost soul.

"The cold wind swept across the plain,
   "And savored of the sea;
"It came from my dear, sunny home,
   "Lost like a dream to me.

"The corpse's pale lips then unenclosed,
   "His teeth in the moonlight shone,
"I sat and wept and beat my breast,
   "Till close upon night's noon.

"Out of the chalice of the east,
    "Dark clouds began to rise,
"Mass upon mass, and broad and fast,
    "Red currents crossed the skies;

"And a moaning sound grew up afar,
    "Like music in the air;
"It circled round and round the dead,
    "And wailed and murmured there;

"A star slid down from heaven's roof,
    "And nestled by his head;
"I knew it was his spirit, come
    "With me to watch the Dead.

"And by its light,—oh, sad, sad sight!
    "Two shadows I could see;
"One sate on either side, both gazed
    "By turns on him and me.

"A soft light from their snowy hair
    "Fell on his dead, pale face;
"They were his mother and his sire,
    "Come from their heavenly place,
"To watch their dead, dead, mangled son,
    "The last of all their race.

"Ah, God! those eyes did search my soul,
  "So calm and sad they were;
"They were a conscience unto me,
  "And yet I could not stir.

"The dark clouds folded over the moon,
  "Like a wild rushing river,
"The lightning in the stormy east
  "From bank to bank did quiver.

"Peal upon peal the thunder spoke,—
  "My soul it did rejoice;
"Me from that death in life it woke,
  "Like an old schoolmate's voice.

"That star still shone, in light or gloom,
  "Like light in a dead man's eye;
"Those white-haired shadows never stirred,
  "But still sat calmly by.

"Again I had the power to move,
  "And I turned away mine eye;
"Between me and the clouds I saw
  "A troop come hurrying by.

"With eager course they, man and horse,
    "Like the wind of a tempest pressed;
"The lightning glittered through their shapes,
    "As it glitters through the mist.

"This shadowy army of the dead,
    "Rushed by me like the wind,
"Before, the thunder-hounds did bay,
    "And a tempest howled behind.

"And, as they swept by me, I knew
    "Each wan and ghastly face;
"Oh, God! how changed, since I and they
    "Began that awful chase!

"The corse's spirit-star was quenched,
    "As they came hurtling past,
"And he uprose as if alive,
    "And before the troop fled fast.

"My hound sprang forward on the track
    "Of the dead, bay after bay,
"My horse, too, joined the spectral host,
    "And madly dashed away.

"All night the fierce storm roared around,
　"And the thunder's constant roll;
"But still the gray-haired shadows' voice,
"Was heard above the tempest's noise,
　"Like moans within the soul.

"And every year, this very night,
　"That chase is held again:
"Again the skeleton flits fast
　"Before that phantom-train.

"And every year, the very day
　. "When we began the chase,
"No matter where my weary heart
　"Has found a resting-place;

"No matter where I dwell, my horse
　"And hound come back to me;
"I can not choose but mount, and thus
　"The horrid hunt have we.

"And here, yea, even here, the chase
　"Fails never to be stopped;
"And here, this day, these mouldering bones,
　"Moss-grown and green, have dropped.

"I am a wretched lonely man,
    "No friend, no home, no God;
"Who many a year, through many a clime,
    "My weary way have trod,—
"Alas! I would that I could lay
    "My head beneath the sod!

"The white hair of those parents lies
    "Like a shadow on my soul;
"In dreams his sightless eyeballs burn
    "My worn heart like a coal.

"I pray to Heaven by night and day,
    "My tears flow like the rain;
"And yet my useless cries procure
    "No peace: I pray in vain.

"I dream that I was once a child,
    "No bird more blithe and gay,
"My young heart, like a honey-bee,
    "That hums the live-long day:
"But now it is a maimed bird,
    "That mourns its life away."

"God help thee, man! Thy crmas great,
    "But in the eye of Heaven,
"Repentance may atone for all,—
    "Thy great sin be forgiven.

"So we must dig a grave, and lay
  "These mouldering bones therein,—
"Perhaps they there may rest, until
  "The great assize begin.

"And we must pray to God on high
  "And his beloved Son,
"To shed their gentle, genial rain
  "Of love thy heart upon.

"So shall thy great sin be atoned,
  "The murdered so forgive;
"And like the dead man touched by Christ,
  "Thou shalt arise and live,"

With sword and battle-axe, the twain
  Full earnestly did work,
While round them from the eastern caves
  Night gathered, thick and mirk.

The moon arose, the gentle stars
  Opened their lustrous eyes;
The spirit-star sate near the dead,
  The shadows came likewise.

Before the moon fared overhead,
   The grave was hollowed deep,
And earnestly they cried to Heaven,
   To pardon and to keep
The soul whose sin had been so great,
   And its remorse so deep.

The Hermit kneeled by the skeleton,
   His thick tears wet the bones,
Like echoes from his inmost soul,
   He uttered earnest moans.

His tears fell on the spirit-star,
   And it blazed like a shaft of fire;
While music stole from the shadows' lips
   Like the murmuring of a lyre.

They laid the bones within the grave,
   They piled the sods thereon
And many a fervent prayer they prayed,
   After this toil was done.

The white star circled thrice around
   The sodded grave above,
And the Hermit felt a load of woe
   From his anguished heart remove;
For the light of the shadows' glittering hair

Sank into his soul and nestled there,
  Like a dream of gentle love.

The moon that stood right overhead,
  Was quenched as 'twere a lamp,
And a cold wind broke, and flitted by,
  Its dark wings chill and damp.

Afar upon the east rang out,
  A wild, fierce, startling bay,
And through the misty fields of foam,
  Careered the wild array.

Till, near the grave, like a rushing wave,
  The spectral huntsmen halt,
And circling round, each shadowy hound
  Bays loudly, as at fault.

The star, arising from the grave,
  Slowly toward Heaven soared,
And from it a great snowy light
  Upon the Hermit poured.

Faint music from the pale, sad lips
  Of the gray-haired shadows stole,
And filled the mute, delighted air,
  And soothed the Hermit's soul.

Shrill cries were heard, the air was stirred,
　　As if wings rustled there,
And the spectral huntsmen melted, like
　　Thin shadows, into air.

Then through the lonely desert rung
　　The Æolian harps of Heaven
And Angel-voices sweetly sung,
　　"The guilty is forgiven;
"Calm, calm thy troubled soul to peace!
　　"Thy chains of woe are riven."

A LAMENT FOR DIXIE.

Southrons, conquered, subjugated,
Mourn your country devastated!
  Mourn for hapless, hopeless Dixie!
Homes once happy, desolated,
Church and altar desecrated;
  Mourn for fallen, ruined Dixie!

      Lament the fall of Dixie!
        Alas! Alas!
     On Dixie's land we'll sadly stand,
      And live or die for Dixie,
        Endure! Endure!
      All ills endure for Dixie!
        Endure! Endure!
      All ills endure for Dixie!

Mourn your dead whose bones lie bleaching,
Courage to the living teaching;
  Wail, but still be proud for Dixie!
Mourn your Southland, crushed and trampled,
Bearing sorrows unexampled;
  Wail, but still be proud for Dixie!
      Lament, etc.

Prey despoiled and victim bleeding,
Not to man for mercy pleading,
    Unto God alone cries Dixie:
Cross of anguish bravely bearing,
Crown of thorns submissive wearing,
    Patient and resigned is Dixie.
        Lament, etc.

All our States lie fainting, dying,
Each to each with sobs replying,
    Each still loving, honoring Dixie:
By the accurst scourge lacerated,
By her freed slaves ruled and hated,
    She is still our own dear Dixie.
        Lament, etc.

Dear to us our conquered banners,
Greeted once with loud hosannas;
    Dear the tattered flag of Dixie:
Dear the field of Honor glorious,
Where, defeated or victorious,
    Sleep the immortal Dead of Dixie.
        Lament, etc.

Conquered, we are not degraded,
Southern laurels have not faded;
    Mourn, but not in shame, for Dixie!
Deck your Heroes' graves with garlands,
Till the echo comes from far lands,
    "Honor to the dead of Dixie!"
        Lament, etc.

All is not yet lost unto us,—
Baseness only can undo us;
    Mourn,—you cannot blush,—for Dixie!
Kneeling at your country's altar,
Swear your children not to falter,
    Till the right shall rule in Dixie.
        Lament, etc.

If her fate be sealed, we'll share it;
By our shroudless dead we swear it;
    Ours the life or death of Dixie!
By her Past's all-glorious story,
By her loyal Martyrs' glory,
    We will live or die with Dixie!
        Lament, etc.

Shall there to our Night of Sorrow
Be no glad or bright To-morrow?
  Is hope, even, lost to Dixie?—
Every dark night hath its morning,
Long, though, oft, delayed its dawning:
  Wait! be patient! pray for Dixie!

           Hope for dawn for Dixie!
             Endure!   Endure!
           On Dixie's land we'll fearless stand,
             And hope and pray for Dixie.
               Endure!   Endure!
             All ills endure for Dixie!
               Endure!   Endure!
             All ills endure for Dixie!

                              1868.

JUBILATE.

Now our night of terror endeth,
God his Rose of Dawn now sendeth,
    Giving life and light to Dixie:
Arms no longer Fraud sustaining,
Knaves and thieves no longer reigning,
    Hope is once more born for Dixie.
      Life has come to Dixie;
          She's free! free!! free!!!—
On Dixie's land we now may stand,
    No longer tortured Dixie:
      She's free! free!! free!!!
Our own, dear, wasted Dixie:
      She's free! free!! free!!!
For God is good to Dixie.

1877.

REFLECTIONS.

The stars shine sweetly in the skies,
    Where, hours ago, they gently stole,
Even as a lady's lovely eyes
    Look in upon her lover's soul:
The murmur of the mighty river,
    Rolls on, a melancholy tune;
Over the eastern mountains quiver
    The first rays of the wasted moon;
    For daylight cometh, ah, too soon,
To end a pleasant night that ought to last forever.

In the dim starlight, all around,
    Sleeps each deserted, lonely street,
Save when, at intervals, resound
    Some watcher's melancholy feet.
High up in heaven one lovely star
    Pours in upon my soul its light;
As, nested from the world afar,
    A dove, with eyes clear, fond, and bright,
    Gazes, with earnest, mute delight,
Upon its young, that all its life and treasure are.

It seems as if the stars could hear,
So soft, so still, so calm it is,
Each footfall, that, distinct and clear,
Rings through the city's passages.
The wild excitement of the day,
Calmed by this sweet night's gentle power,
Like a strange dream has passed away,
And now at this late, silent hour,
The heart expands, as does a flower,
Fed by the light and dew of a soft morn in May.

The snows of Time fall cold upon
The fountains that well up within
The boyish heart, and mock the sun
With their bright, bubbling, merry din.
There comes no joyous summer-rain,
That can unlock these frozen springs;
Nor can the southern breeze again
Release them with its sunny wings:
The icy mass that round them clings,
Through life's long winter grows, and growing doth remain.

Now the thick stars grow pale, and fade
　　Before the moon's unclouded brow,
Whose light, encroaching on gray shade,
　　Sleeps like a drift of mountain-snow.
How trivial now appear the fret
　　And fever of this busy life!
The cares and troubles that beset,
　　The madness of this party-strife,
　　Wherewith all hearts are now so rife,
That even I, who blame, feel the wild fever yet.

But tree and leaf and bud and flower
　　Speak with a language eloquent;
And soothed by them and this sweet hour,
　　I feel how vainly life is spent;
How wretched and degrading all
　　This toil for power and office is,
In which one needs must crouch and crawl
　　If he expect or hope success;
　　The unwashed feet of thousands kiss,
And grovelling before strange idols prostrate fall.

How little do mankind commune
  With NATURE, or the truths regard,
Whereof, at all times, night or noon,
  Her student reaps a rich reward!
We scarcely glance at that great book,
  Whose bright leaves ever open lie;
Nor therein for instruction look,
  With calm and philosophic eye.
  Alas! that we should live and die
As if mankind no more of aught divine partook.

Out on this wretched party-war!
  Where the best weapons, trick, chicane,
And perjury and cunning are,—
  Its picked troops, scoundrelism's train,—
Where baser men outweigh the best,
  Lies always over truth prevail,
Wisdom by numbers is oppressed,
  Knavery at Virtue dares to rail,
  Slanders the brightest name assail;—
Victory in such a war humbles the victor's crest.

Henceforth, myself I dedicate
    To other service.   Let me read
Thy pages, NATURE!—though so late
    Thy voice of reprimand I heed.
From bud and leaf, from flower and bloom,
    From every fair created thing,
Thy teachings will my soul illume,
    So long in darkness slumbering;
    That when to Life's bright sunny Spring,
Autumn succeeds, it may not all my hopes entomb.

My children, with their innocent looks,
    My home, with modest, humble cheer,
My old, familiar, friendly books,
    Companions faithful and sincere?—
What want I more, if I am wise,
    To cheer me on my quiet way?
Honor and fame no more I prize,—
    Let those THAT harvest reap who may.—
    But lo! Dawn heralds blushing Day,
And now, contentedly, I close my weary eyes.

1844.

RE-UNION.

Let us drink, together, fellows, as we did in days of yore,
And still enjoy the golden hours that Fortune has in store,
The absent friends remembered be, in all that's sung or said,
And Love immortal consecrate the memory of the dead.

Fill every goblet to the brim!—let every heart be filled
With kindly recollections, and all bitter ones be stilled!
Come round me, dear old fellows, and in chorus as we sing,
Life's Autumn days shall be as glad as were its days of Spring.

Drink, Brothers, to the absent who are living, first of all,
While each familiar name and face we lovingly recall!
The generous and brave and good! The kind, and frank,
    and true,
Who knew not how false word to speak or what was base to
    do.

We see the faces of the Dead; they hover in the air,
And looking on us lovingly, our mirth they seem to share;
O dearly loved! though ye have gone to other stars or
    spheres,
We still have for you thoughts of love and consecrated tears.

225

Pour a libation rich with love upon the graves that hold
The ashes of the gallant hearts that long ago grew cold;
And swear that never party feuds or civil war shall break
Our bonds of love, and enemies of friends and comrades make.

The Dead are with us always, friends! let us their teachings
    heed!
"Forgive thy brother, if he err!" they eloquently plead:
"Let bygones be bygones!" they cry; "let the old love revive!
"And on the altars of your hearts keep Friendship's fire
    alive."

It is better far to love than hate, for Nations as for men;
Let us hope the good old humour soon will bless the land
    again:
But if the politicians still would wrangle, scold, and fight,
Their quarrels shall not break the ties that we re-knit to-
    night.

Our Autumn days of life have come, the frosts begin to fall,
Beyond the dark, deep river, hark! we hear old comrades call.
To the Dead and Living whom each loves, let each his goblet
    fill;
And the memory of the dead shall make the living dearer still.

Washington, January, 1869.

NIGHT.

A REVERIE.

I can not sleep; for many a dream of home
Through the dark caverns of the brain has come,
Peopling its desert with bright images
Of all that I have left or lost: there is
No sleep for me; and I will walk awhile.
'Tis midnight, and the thick stars brightly smile
Upon the slumbering earth; the deep clear stream
Glides noiseless by my feet; the still world dreams
Of its age of gold, long vanished. All around
The listening ear detects no passing sound,
Save the wild wolf's cry, that among far hills,
Afflicts night's ear with long, low, mournful thrills;
And the hoarse owl, that now and then booms out
His harsh, unearthly melancholy shout,
And then is silent; while at intervals,
The watch-dog moans, and stirs, and once more falls
Into deep slumber. Still as infant death,
The broad and heavy forest sleeps beneath
The white foam of the Galaxy, which lies
Above its green waves, with its myriad eyes,
Patiently shining from its silver drifts.
No wind his wild and mournful voice uplifts,
Among the tree-tops; everything lies still.

Now is the hour for thought; the mind can fill
Itself with voices at this solemn hour.
The thoughts so dormant under daylight's power,
Like wingless bees, swarming about the heart,
With wild, uncertain, troubled melody,
Are shaped by midnight's calm, resistless art,
To forms that, coming from the shadowy sea
Of memory, people the quivering soul.
The echoes of the past roll through the heart,
With palpable and strange reality,
And shake its strings, as the wind shakes the chords
Of an Æolian harp, till from its roll
The keen vibrations of intensest thought.
The soul now wanders back to its old home,
And flits through every well-remembered spot,
Where I was used in olden times to roam;
And peers in many a much-loved face, that not
A thousand years could from my heart erase:
Wanders beneath old trees, by rustic wells,
And quaint old houses hidden in low dells,
And ancient orchards of old mossy trees,
And wheat-fields waving in the summer breeze,
And rude old bridges, spanning clear blue streams,
And many a lilied pond that idly dreams
Under great trees; so that, for some small space,
I leave this wild uncultivated place,
And am again, oh, blessed word! a boy:

The golden wings of peace, contentment, joy,
Wave over me again, and soothe the soul,
Hushing the passions I can not control.

NIGHT! Thou art lovely and magnificent,
When down from heaven thou silently hast leant,
Soothing earth, sea, and sky to gentle sleep,
While summer-clouds and stars their watches keep.
.Night! I have watched thee many a weary hour;
I have stood high on earthquake-rifted tower
Of granite mountain, in eternal snow,
And there have worshipped thee, and bended low
Before thy presence. Then thy stars were cold
And glittering, as the bright and heartless world.
Then sometime thou didst hang thy silver lamp
On the sky's wall; and like white flags unfurled,
Around the blue heaven's star-tented camp,
The clouds shook in the wind, and with soft light
Thou fed'st thy lamp. Over unbounded plains,
The wolf-heart Indian's broad and dry domains,
I have beheld thee in thy every guise,
Where thy caress has often soothed mine eyes
To quiet sleep upon the rugged ground,
And now, O Queen! as thus I pace around,
Holding with thee this converse, thou dost seem
To speak to me, like voices in a dream.

Is it the tree-tops moaning their low dirge?
The sweet, soft murmuring of the air-sea's surge
Among their tremulous leaves? Oh, no: it is
Thy spirit whispering to the charmed trees,
And thus it findeth words:

The stars are mine; and when I rise
To bless the weary earth and skies,
Then they lift up their lids of blue,
And gladly gleam heaven's black robes through.

Their radiant eyes, that were quenched all day
By the tyrant sun, at my coming gray
Are lighted, and sparkle with glee again,
Until at the dawn my dark tides wane.

The woods are mine, when they sleep so still,
That their pulses hardly throb or thrill:
And when their hearts, deep, dark, and dim,
Are stirred, and sing their awful hymn.

The sea is mine, when the thick stars lie
On its calm breast and wink at the sky;
Or tempest frets it into waves,
And shakes the dead in their deep-sea graves.

The mountains are mine,—each snowy cone
That lifts like a prayer toward God's high throne;
And every cavern, dark and mirk
As those where the murderer does his work.

The mountains are mine,—around their peaks
I wrap my wings while the lightning leaks
From the gaping rifts of the thunder-rack,
And the starry snow has become jet-black.

The plains are mine, when they sleep as still
As a child that just has gained his will;
When I lift to the gale my broad, black sail,
And the winds behind my storm-ship wail.

The earth is mine, for my foe, the sun,
Continually circling her, runs on:
For many a long and weary age,
The sun and I our conflict wage:

And I am to overtake him yet,
When the earth will see his last long set:
When he will be quenched upon her brink,
And she will back to chaos sink.

Then will I reign for ever and ever,
When the stars are all sunk in heaven's river;—
It has been once,—it shall be again,—
For time even now begins to wane.

I am a portion of chaos, left
For long years over the earth to drift;
At times to be full of peace and calm;
Then alive with the lightning and thunder-psalm.

The earth will be my slave again,
But my victory will be all in vain;
There will be a brighter and better sphere,
Which I can never come anear.

While I shall hold Creation's shell,
Her myriad souls, I know full well,
Out of her cold, deep heart will rise,
And float like stars up to unseen skies.

And while over chaos and ruin I brood,
In the purple glooms of my solitude,
In heaven will God's great loving eye
Be the sun of a day that will never die.

1833.

AN INVITATION.

Come out and sit with me, dear wife, beneath these branch-
    ing trees,
And let our little children come, and clamber on our knees!
It is a sweet, soft, pleasant morn, the loveliest in May,
And their little hearts are beating fast, longing to be at play.

The shadows here are thick and cool, the south wind stirs
    the leaves,
The martin sings a merry note upon the ivied eaves;
The crisp grass wears a richer green, from yesterday's soft
    showers,
And is jewelled over thickly with the rarest of your flowers.

The odors of the jasmine and the roses fill the air,
And the bees, refreshed by Night's sweet rest, again begin
    to bear
Rich freightage to their palaces under the locust trees,
Rejoicing in the influence of this sweet summer breeze.

The humming-birds are busy through the flower-encum-
    bered vines,
Where the golden honeysuckle, from our own green woods,
    entwines
With its paler foreign sisters, 'mid whose dark-green, glossy
    leaves
The flowers profusely clustered there entice the tiny thieves.

233

Where the coral woodbine flauntingly displays its crimson
   blooms,
And our native yellow jasmine pours abroad its rich per-
   fumes;
Where the climbing roses cluster, painted rich with every hue,
And stem, and leaf, and bud, and flower, are glittering with
   dew.

A hundred snowy doves upon the grass have settled down,
Like a drift of stainless snow upon a green hill's sunny crown;
They wait to be, as usual, by our little children fed,
Who, idle ones, are playing here, under the trees, instead.

The mocking-bird, for many a week so busy, now can rest,
For yesterday I saw him give the last touch to his nest;
His eyes shine brightly now with joy, his songs rings loud
   and shrill;
Now here, now there, in mad delight, he's not a moment
   still.

Behold! just overhead, his mate is sitting on the nest,
You can see above its edges, the gray feathers of her breast,
Ah, happy bird!—but we, dear wife, are happier than she;
For OUR young carol round us now, in childhood's merry glee.

The sun's first rays are shooting up above the eastern woods;
But here, among these circled trees, no prying light intrudes:

Five sturdy oaks are ranged around; five children round us
    throng.
And after each we'll name a tree, that shall to each belong.

This tallest one for HAMILTON, our little manly boy,
Whose dark and thoughtful eyes are now so radiant with joy;
This, WALTER'S, whose bright, dancing ones with merry
    mischief shine,
But still, affectionate and kind, are images of thine.

This, for our silent little girl, the quiet ISADORE,
Who sits demurely working at her doll's new pinafore;
This, for our blue-eyed LILIAN, the merriest of all;
This smallest, for the babe, that by his father's name we call.

Life's spring has passed from us, dear wife; its summer glides
    away,
And melancholy autumn comes, robed in its vesture gray;
We may linger on till winter; we may die before we are old;
But these young oaks will live and thrive when we are dead
    and cold.

We have been very happy, dear, for more than ten long
    years:—
How short, as we look backward, that long space of time
    appears!

And if these dear ones all are spared, around our hearts to
    cling,
The autumn of our life will be as happy as its spring.

For many a pleasant year, perhaps, to bless us, they may live,
Kind solace and assistance to our feeble age to give;—
May help us totter out beneath these interlocking trees,
Enjoying, as life fades away, the pleasant morning breeze.

We will make them virtuous, honest, true, kind, generous;
    and when
They are grown to lovely women, and true-hearted, gallant
    men,
Then, having done our duty, we, without a tear or sigh,
With cheerful resignation may be well content to die.

And after we are dead and gone, and buried many a year,
They, with THEIR children gathered round, may sit as we
    do here;
New flowers will bloom around them then, though these,
    like us, will fade;
But the green oaks we planted still will bless them with their
    shade.

Then will they think of us, dear wife, with love and grief
    sincere,
And sadly on our memory bestow a silent tear;
Let this our consolation be, while life shall swiftly wane,—
In our sweet children's virtues we shall live and love again.

236

MORNING.

A Lament

I.

The dew steeps the heart of the flower,
   And the green bending rays of the grass,
And there, in an unseen shower,
   The mist and sweet odors mass:
The sensitive plant of the bosom,
   Is quivering, shrinking, and pale;
No dews feed its withering blossom,
   Winds through its parched leaves wail.

II.

The fast stream that runs from the mountain,
   Is wreathing its white brow with mist;
And its edge, like the brim of a fountain,
   With grass and sweet flowers is kissed:
The waves of the heart's crimson river
   Flow on, uncrowned with light;
The weeds on its dark banks shiver,
   And shrink from the roar of its flight.

237

III.

The sunshine is cradled in leaves,
   And rocked by the unseen air,
While the sea of emerald heaves,
   With a slumberous motion there:
No cheerful sunshine sleeps
   In the dark caves of the soul,
But the sad heart ever weeps
   For a grief beyond control.

IV.

Morn's purple and crimson torrent,
   Upon the mountain pours;
And still amid that current,
   The sunlight rains its showers:
The fire of passion blazes,
   Less hotly than of old;
And sorrow, like sea-mist, chases
   The morning's purple and gold.

V.

The eagle sits on his eyrie,
  A golden haze round him clings,
On a pyramid lone and dreary
  He fans the snow with his wings:
The eagle Ambition remaineth,
  Fanning the icy heart;
His keen eye never waneth,
  Till the soul and its frail house part.

VI.

The thrush on his nest is brooding,
  His wings slowly winnow the air,
And a sea of music is flooding
  The great green forest there:
No cheerful song is ringing
  Through the sad heart's solitude;
Nor birds of joy soft-singing,
  Among its ruins brood.

VII.

The influence of the morning
　　Is sweet after the recent rain;
To the heart it is only a warning,
　　That night will come again:
The heart was once all glory
　　Till boyhood faded away;
Its course is now the story
　　Of an evanescent day.

VIII.

The spirit of morning burneth
　　On his altar orient;
But the glooms that the sea inurneth,
　　At night will be unpent:
The spirit of life is fainting,
　　Pressed by the glooms of death;
Like moonlight on a painting,
　　Life merely lingereth.

240

IX.

A shadow is on the soul,
　　Like a shadow on the sea;
Though the songs of glory roll
　　With a grave sublimity:
　Like a current of pale moonlight,
　　In the light of a flickering lamp,
A light like shadow, half dark, half bright,
　　Is life in this earthly camp.

X.

Pale Death is bending over
　　The worn and weary heart;
Ah, what a constant lover,
　　Grim Emperor, thou art!—
The soft, faint light of sorrow
　　Shines on the wasted scroll;
It will close, and the lamps go out to-morrow;
　　The arrow is near its goal.

1835.

MIDNIGHT.

A Lament.

I.

The stars are massing in heaven,
   Lid after lid they unfold;
But the showers of light that are given
   To the earth are frosty and cold:
The light of each earthly star,
   Of Fortune, Honor and Fame,
Is shining brightly afar,
   But cold to the heart is their flame.

II.

The moon sitteth on the mountain,
   Like a golden eagle alit
By the brim of a foaming fountain,
   Where his wings with the spray are wet;
The moonlight of friendship has vanished,
   From the crags that shadow my way,
The stars from my heaven are banished,
   And wander sadly away.

III.

The cold wind wails through the flower,
  Shaking its leaves to the ground,
And the grass receives the shower
  With a melancholy sound:
The flowers of joy are shattered
  By sorrow's tyrannous air,
And their crimson leaves are watered
  By the night-dew of despair.

IV.

The sphered Venus resteth
  Upon a western cone,
And coldly she investeth
  With light her icy throne:
The sphered light of Love
  Revolves within the heart,
And its wasting fountains move
  With a convulsive start.

V.

The shadows of the ridges
    Are massed upon the plain,
And there, from withered sedges,
    The dying winds complain
The heavy shades of anguish
    Are massed upon the soul,
And there the death-notes languish,
    And through its desert roll.

VI.

The snowy tents are sleeping
    Upon the dusky prairie,
Like white-winged eagles, keeping
    Watch over their lonely eyrie:
The shadows of the Past
    Are sitting by my side;
The world is else a vast,
    And I with them abide.

VII.

Thin spheres of dew are raining,
  Unseen, in the moonlit air;
And the grass, when night is waning,
  Bright crowns of frost will wear;
Death-frosts are swiftly chilling
  The pulses of the heart;
Slow, slow the harp is thrilling,—
  Its harmonies depart.

VIII.

The clouds are slowly steering
  Their fleets around the moon;
Amid them she is veering,
  To vanish, ah! too soon!—
The moonlight of existence
  Is flickering and pale:
And darkly, in the distance,
  Death spreads his shadowy sail.

IX.

The soul is slowly moaning
   Her sad and stern lament;
Decay is fast dethroning
   The passions Heaven lent:
Death's steps are sadly echoing
   Its wasted cells within;
Far in its deepest caves they ring,
   With melancholy din.

X.

The eagle, proudly soaring,
   Mourns not the fleeting night,
When, on the mountains pouring,
   Awakes the red daylight:
Why mourn this dream of Life
   When happily 'tis waning,
And on its clouds of strife
   The light of Death is raining?

1835.

THE FALL OF POLAND.

She has sunken again into slavery's tomb,
  Like a thunderbolt quenching itself in the sea;
And deeply and darkly engraved is her doom,—
  "Her existence is done!   Let her never be free!"

From the darkness that long eddied round her she rose,
  And flinging her grave-clothes of bondage aside,
A brave, bold defiance she hurled at her foes;
  And her shot-riddled flag flew once more in its pride.

'Twas the battle of RIGHT against Outrage and Wrong,
  The last noble struggle for life and free laws;
And every heart to whose feelings belong
  Any generous impulses, prayed for her cause.

As the clouds of a tropical hurricane roll
  From horizon to zenith, so swelled her array;
As the broad fields of ice drifting south from the pole,
  So gathered her forces, all fierce for the fray.

For each manly heart in which beat the free blood
    Of a true Polack joyfully rushed to the ranks;
Then forth to the frontier they rolled, like a flood
    That, swelled with great rains, overflows all its banks.

And lo! the old flag proudly waved in the air,
    Over city and plain, as of yore was its wont;
And the souls of her mighty departed were there,
    Like the shades of dead gods, marching on in the front.

But the fetters are clasped on her limbs once again,
    And riveted strongly, and clenched there forever;
Sad, sad, is her soul, sharp and bitter her pain,
    And dark the deep dungeons where light wandereth never.

Oh, shame on you! shame on you, children of Gaul!
    You had just become free, and you might have been great;
But you suffered the noblest of nations to fall,
    And lie bleeding and maimed at the merciless gate

Of the grim Northern Wolf, whose white teeth, dripping red,
    Yet mangle the corpse of the stag he has slain.
Shame! shame! a proud people were better be dead,
    Than disgraced by ingratitude's ignoble stain.

When a word from your mouth, like the lightning's swift
      flame,
  Would have sent back the Wolf to his lair in the snow,
And made the dull hater of Freedom as tame
  As his serfs, that smile thanks in return for a blow.

When you might have been hailed the true kings of the
      world,
  And your memory ever regarded with love;
Had you struck but one blow, but one cannon-shot hurled,
  The thunders of God would have helped from above.

That then you should heed not their earnest appeal,
  Who under Napoleon fought by your side,
Nor think that you saw, through the glitter of steel,
  Brave Poniatowski rejoicingly ride!

Live on, then, and crouch to your Citizen King!
  This tale of your baseness shall often be sung;
And its memory, a halo of shame, round you cling,
  To be never thrown off while the world has a tongue.

1832.

FRANCE.

Wake! children of France! shall your tyrant forever
   Enslave and enchain you, and trample you down?
Do you fear the sharp fetters that gall you to sever,
   And tear from the brow of the despot his crown?

Up! children of France!　Let the flag that you honor,
   Be once more the flag of the free and the brave!
Your country is chained; the Philistines are on her;
   Who heeds not her call is both coward and knave.

If you have but one spark of the spirit that lighted
   The souls of your fathers, exhibit it now;
And sheathe not the sword till your wrongs are all righted,
   Though blood to the reins of your horses should flow.

Ye fear not the throne, nor its base truckling minions;
   On, on to the contest with cuirass and lance!
Till your eagles again spread their conquering pinions,
   And peace and security reign over France.

Let the pale monarchs quake! for their thrones shall be
       shaken!
  Let them league once again, as they leagued once before!
Their fury and madness, when France shall awaken,
   Will be like the ocean-wave chafing the shore.

250

Up! men of gay France!—Your poor children upbraid you,
　　Your gray-headed parents cry out on your shame;
Up! up! and your ancestors' spirits will aid you,
　　Your tyrant to humble, your taskmaker tame.

Strike, children of France! strike for freedom and glory,
　　As ye and your fathers have stricken before;
Ye may fall, but your names shall be blazoned in story,
　　To beacon the free through the hurricane's roar.

Black Eagle of Russia! thy pride shall be lowered,
　　When France and her armies are roused for the fray;
And Austria shall cower again, as she cowered
　．When the Corsican swept her great armies away.

Up! arm for the contest!　Your foes are around you;
　　The foot of your king presses hard on your hearts;
The Pigmies came, while you were sleeping, and bound you:
　　Strike once, ere occasion forever departs!

One blow! but one blow!—for your long years of anguish!
　　Your children, your parents, your own honest fame!
Or will you through ages of agony languish,—
　　To be cowards at heart.　Frenchmen only in name?

　　　　　　　　　　　　　　1829.

SHELLEY.

Only a few short years ago, there sat
A youth on one of old Rome's seven hills,
Beneath a ruined temple, and upon
A broken fragment of a marble column.
Around the stern and silent ruins cast
Their massive shadows, and a tangled maze
Of trees, and flowers, and shrubs, was rich along
The face of the declivity.   The sun
Was setting upon Rome; and through the clouds
His glorious spirit revelled, lighting up
Their fluctuating drifts with all his hues
Of placid melancholy, and the deep
Calm beauty of a soft Italian eve.
Below him lay the city:—beautiful!
Dome, palace, spire, all radiant with the glow
And perfect beauty of that hour of peace.

  The time accorded with his soul,—that deep,
Abundant fountain of impassioned thought,
Which the world in vain had striven to choke up.
He came from England there, to feed his soul
With inspiration from those mighty ruins,
And to escape the cold, offensive sneer
And hatred of the world.   Alas! he erred;
His dark and dreary creed was one that awes
All hearts that worship in our sacred faith.

Yet we should rather pity than condemn
The blind of heart, even as the blind of eye.
His pen, too bold, had warred with our belief:
His name was written on the traveller's page
On St. Bernard; and also, underneath,
With his own hand, the sad word, "*Atheos.*"

But he was moral, generous, pure of heart,
Gentle and kind as any innocent child;
And he was persecuted, and so fled.
The world, that should by kindest means have striven
To wean so fine a soul from its mad creed,
Had hunted him, and tortured his kind heart,
With calumny and hatred, as it ever
Hunts those who contravene its cherished faith.
This was not all; but poverty had worn,
Like a cold iron, to his soul. Oh, world!
Thou knowest not how many glorious sons
Of Poetry thy hard, cold heart has left
To faint and languish, with a living death!
He sat and mused, soothing his constant pain
With soft, sweet fancies, of the sunset born.
His melancholy wove its lovely thoughts
Into rich words, brilliantly beautiful,
Colored like one of Titian's masterpieces,
Or Guido's lovely faces. All his sorrows
Couched in his soul, and only tinged his verse
With imperceptible tints. His lovely songs

253

Were paintings,—masses of rich, glowing words,
Full of sweet feeling, and a singular power.
Like his own sky-lark, up at Heaven's gate,
Above the earth and all its meaner things,
He sang, and soared higher than mortal ken.
But at rare times a sudden thought would shoot,
Like a sharp pang of bitter agony,
Through his wronged heart, and dim the vivid fire
Of lofty thoughts and noble aspirations.
Then would he drop his pen. His slender form,
Attenuated, slight, ethereal, shook
With the vibrations of his spirit, Then
The fine, transparent, delicate, boyish face
Became still paler and more spiritual;
And the clear eye, that did relieve that look
Of boyishness, with its soft, brilliant light,
Contracted with a sudden spasm of pain:—
That eye, within whose wondrous depths you saw
The soul itself,—so tender, yet intense,
So bright and keen, and yet so melancholy.
But this went by; and conquering his sorrow,
He wrote again. Is it not very strange
How the strong soul can pour its golden thoughts,
Its musical words and bright imaginings
In the world's ear, when round it lies the wreck
Of many hopes; when the poor, throbbing heart
Is weary of its struggle, and would fain

254

Lie down and sleep in that most peaceful couch,
Where ghastly dreams come not,—the quiet grave?
It is a sad, sweet pleasure to the heart
To watch its own decline. It wastes away,
But burns the brighter as it suffers more.
Perhaps to him his poetry, indeed,
Was its own sweet reward. As though we shared
Our secret sorrow with some dear old friend,
We do commune most intimately with
Our inmost heart; and all our deeper thoughts,
Which we could not have spoken, we can write:—
Not to display them to the world, but like
A man who, sitting by his fireside, talks,
Of a sharp winter night, with one who went
To school with him through many a drift of snow,
When they were careless and contented boys.
And he who terms this egotism, knows
No more the nature of a Poet's soul
Than do the stupid beasts that chew the cud.
Not many moons had changed, when SHELLEY sailed
On the calm sea that washes the fair shores
Of sunny Italy. Long hours he lay,
Leaving his boat to wander where it listed,
While all the memories of his past life floated,
Like memories of dreams, before his eyes.

The scene was changed. Clouds, wind, storm, rain, and fire,
Howled angrily along the startled sea;
Blue lightning hissed upon the crested waves;
Winds from the bending forests on the shore
Lashed the mad waters. Still, through all the storm,
He had the same calm, spiritual look,
The same clear, bright, yet melancholy eye,
As when among the ruins of old Rome.
Perhaps there was a sick throb of the heart;—
A wish to win, before he died, more fame,
And some small portion of earth's happiness.

But who shall tell his thoughts? Perhaps he then
Doubted the truth of his dark, cheerless creed,
And shrank in horror from oblivion,
Decomposition, death, annihilation.—
Perhaps!—
    The frail bark foundered, and the waves
Quenched a great light and left the world to mourn.
It is enough to make the poet sick
Of his high art, and scorn the clamorous world,
And life, and fame, that guerdon dearly won
By broken hopes, sad days, and early death,
When he remembers the short, bitter life.
And sad end of poor SHELLEY.

        Fare thee well,
Young star of poetry, now set forever!
Yet, though eclipsed forever to this world,

Still thy light fills the earth's dull atmosphere,
A legacy inestimable. Man
Hath done thee wrong, wronging himself the more,
By cold neglect, and small appreciation
Of thy divinest songs. The day will come
When justice will be done thee. Adonais,
The bound Prometheus, will become great lamps
Lit on the edges of thick darkness, blazing
Over broad lands and out on weltering seas,
Like glorious suns that midnight change to noon:
Great beacons on the fringes of the sea,
Speaking the glories of the hoary Past
To future ages, far in the womb of Time,
And flashing inspiration on that sea,
And all the earnest souls that journey there.
Then none of all the muse's younger sons
Will rival thee, except that glorious one,
Who burned thy corpse on Italy's fair shores.
But what is fame to thee? Small recompense
For persecution, obloquy, and wrong;
For poverty and shattered hopes, and life
Embittered till it was no pain to die!

1835.

HYMN.

Awake! awake   Hear Freedom calling
    Upon her sons to fly to arms;
While treason's trumpet-tongue appalling
    Is madly sounding its alarms.
Behold the traitors darkly scheming,
    While Anarchy awakes again,
    Within the darkness of whose brain
Red crime and perjury are teeming.

     To arms! to arms! ye brave;
       The avenging sword unsheath!
       March on! march on! all hearts resolved
       On victory or death!

Is there a heart that now will falter?
    Live, base, ignoble heart, in chains!
Live, with low demagogues to palter!
    Disgrace the free blood in your veins!
Is there a man that strikes not for us,
    Within the shade of Freedom's throne?
    Pale traitor, recreant! fly, and moan
In Slavery's iron realm of horrors!

       To arms, etc.

Traitors and lunatics are aiming
　　To break the Union's golden chain;
Secession's fires are fiercely flaming,
　　And Freedom's heart is racked with pain.
Her eye grows dim, her cheek is paling;
　　And shall we tamely sit and smile,
　　While Treason's feet our land defile,
And Anarchy is loudly railing?

　　　　　To arms, etc.

Shall even our children execrate us,
　　That we have reared them to be slaves?
Our fathers' mouldering bones upbraid us,
　　Stirring in their deep, narrow graves?
Our wives and mothers hate and spurn us,
　　As basest of the base? No! no!
　　To liberty or death we go;
Free let them bless, or corses mourn us!

　　　　　To arms, etc.

Oh, sainted sires! look down upon us,
    And aid us to defend the high
And sacred heritage ye won us!
    Freemen we'll live, or freemen die.
The stars and stripes are floating o'er us;
    Our fathers' spirits lead the front;
    We welcome the fierce battle's brunt:—
Treason and crime shall flee before us!

    To arms, etc.

DISUNION.

Ay, shout! 'Tis the day of your pride,
    Ye despots and tyrants of earth!
Tell your serfs the American name to deride,
    And to rattle their fetters in mirth.
Ay, shout! for the league of the Free
    Is about to be shivered to dust,
And the rent limbs to fall from the vigorous tree,
    Wherein Liberty put her firm trust.
Shout! shout! for more firmly established will be
Your thrones and dominions beyond the blue sea.

Laugh on! for such folly supreme
    The world had yet never beheld;
And ages to come will the history deem
    A tale by antiquity swelled:
For nothing that Time has upbuilt
    And set in the annals of crime,
So stupid and senseless, so wretched in guilt,
    Darkens sober tradition or rhyme.
It will be, like the fable of Eblis' fall,
A byword of mocking and horror to all.

Ye mad, who would raze out your name

From the League of the Proud and the Free,

And a pitiful, separate sovereignty claim,

Like a lone wave flung from off the sea;

Oh, pause ere you plunge into the chasm,

That yawns in your traitorous way!

Ere Freedom, convulsed with one terrible spasm,

Desert you forever and aye!

Pause! think! ere the earthquake astonish your soul,

And the thunders of war through your green valleys roll!

Good God! what a title, what name

Will History give to your crime!

In the deepest abyss of dishonor and shame,

Ye will writhe till the last hour of time;

As braggarts who forged their own chains,

Pulled down what their brave fathers built,

And tainted the blood in their children's young veins

With the poison of slavery and guilt:

And Freedom's bright heart be hereafter, tenfold,

For your folly and fall more discouraged and cold.

What flag shall float over the fires

And the smoke of your patricide war,

Instead of the stars and broad stripes of your sires?

A lone, pale, dim, flickering star,

With a thunder-cloud veiling its glow
    As it faints away into the sea:
Will the Eagle's wing shelter and shield you? Ah, no!
    His wing shelters only the free.
Miscall it, disguise it, boast, rant as you will,
You are traitors, misled by your mad leaders still.

Turn, turn then! Cast down in your might
    The pilots that sit at the helm;
Steer, steer your proud ship from the gulf which dark night
    And treason and fear overwhelm!
Turn back!—From your mountains and glens,
    From your swamps, from the rivers and sea;
From forest and precipice, cavern and den,
    Where your brave fathers bled to be free,
From the graves where those glorious patriots lie,
Re-echoes the warning, "Turn back, or ye die!"

1834.

STANZAS TO ANN.

The spirit in my soul hath woken,
    And bids me speak to thee again;
And silence, many a day unbroken,
    Must cease, although it cease in vain.
As life approaches to its goal,
    And other passions seem to die,
The thoughts of thee that haunt the soul.
    Decay not, sleep not, death defy.

Love's busy wings delight to fan
    A heart that hath been worn to ashes,
And, aided by thy spirit, Ann,
    Beneath his eye that heart still flashes.
Oh! why doth Love build up his nest
    A ruined palace aye within,
Hiding within the poet's breast—
    Why seeks he not a home more green?

He hath no alcyon power, to still
    The passions of the trampled heart,
Rob of its pain the torture-thrill,
    Bid sorrow, want, and pain depart:
Oh no! he adds a fiercer pang
    To every wo which rankles there,
Sharpens the scorpion's fiery fang,
    Adds wildness unto terror's glare.

Yet still, I love thee, and forever—
 No matter what or where I be;
The blow which shall existence sever,
 Alone can end my love for thee.
I love thee as men love but once—
 As few have loved, can love a woman
It seemeth strange, this perfect trance
 Of love, for one that is but human.

But thou wast rich, and I was poor;
 I never spake my love to thee;
And I could all my wo endure,
 Nor ask thee, Ann, to wed with me.
To wed with me!—it were to wed
 With Poverty, and Want, and Wo:
Rather than this, from thee I fled,
 And still a lonely outcast go.

But day by day my love hath grown
 For thee, as all things else decline;
And when I seem the most alone,
 Thy spirit doth commune with mine.
I have no portion with the world,
 Nor hath the world a part with me;
But the lone wave, now shoreward hurled,
 Will turn, yea, dying, turn to thee.

I make to thee, thy love, no claim;
    I ask thee but, when I shall die,
To lay the world-forgotten name
    Within thy heart, and o'er it sigh.
Think that the love which I have felt,
    To which existence hath been given,
Has been as pure as stars that melt
    And die within the depths of heaven.

Fare thee well—it is forever!
    Thou hast heard my dying words;
Till the cords of life shall sever,
    Till the serpent Wo, that girds
The exile heart, its strings have broken,
    Bruised and crushed and shattered it;
Until this, to thee are spoken
    All my words—my dirge is writ.

Arkansas Territory, April 20, 1833.

MY SISTER.

And thou, too, dearest sister! thou art dead!
The pitiless archer once again has sped
At our small circle an unerring dart.
Thus, one by one, alas! from me depart
The images that, in fond memory stored,
I count, as jealous misers count their hoard.
The first fierce stroke the trembling heart that crushed,
The first wild feelings through the brain that rushed,
Are gone, and grief has now become more mild,
For I have wept, as though I were a child,—
I; who had thought my heart contained no tear.
I have returned from deserts wide and drear,
Prairie and snow and mountain eminent,
To hear that it has been thy lot to die,
To feel the snapping of another tie,
One of the few that bound me to the world.
For thou, whose lovely spirit now has furled
Its radiant wings, and folded close therein
Sleeps soundly in the grave, until the din
Of the archangel's mighty trump shall break
The silence of all sepulchres, and wake
All souls upon the resurrection morning;—thou
Didst ever love and trust in me, and now

Thy memory indeed is very dear;
My grief for thee most bitter and sincere.
Ah, heavy loss! ah, great calamity!
How sharp the blow that fate hath struck at me!
When I have climbed the slopes of the great mountains,
Where from eternal snows break out clear fountains,
That grow to mighty rivers; when my feet
Have bled and frozen, and the storms have beat
Upon me pitilessly; when my head
Has made the ground, the rock, the snow its bed,
And I have watched the cold stars stare above:
Then my great solace was my sister's love.
When I have felt most sad and most alone,
When I have walked through multitudes and known
No one that I could greet for olden time;
Or in those spacious solitudes sublime
That flank the Cordilleras; when, among
Their crags the war-whoop in my ears has rung:
When I have fancied I was quite forgot
By ancient friends, my name remembered not,
My features even forgotten, as the dead
When once they slumber in their narrow bed
Pass from men's memories in a day or two:
Then has my wearied soul flown homeward, through
The mist, and darkness; and in most intense

And passionate sorrow, thy proud confidence,
Thy love and faith my comforters have been,
And weaned me from myself and from my spleen.
Ah! sister dear! I have lost thee! thou art gone!
But yet thou hast not left me quite alone.
Perhaps before death closes my worn eyes,
I may again look on New England skies,
Weep at the graves, that like a miser's hoard,
Hold all my wealth, the loved and the adored;
And if, perchance, some one or two are left,
World-wanderers, by tyrannous Fate bereft
Of all that makes us loth with life to part,—
Mother or sister,—take them to my heart,
Shield them, protect them, so that when I die,
Some one above the truant's grave may sigh.

1833.

Made in the USA
Charleston, SC
31 July 2015